MW01077500

Rebecca

REBECCA:
A Father's Journey from Grief to Gratitude

Robert A. Jonas

A Crossroad Book
The Crossroad Publishing Company
New York

1996
The Crossroad Publishing Company
370 Lexington Avenue, New York, NY 10017

Printed in the United States of America

Library of Congress Cataloging-in-Publication Data

Jonas, Robert A.
    Rebecca : a father's journey from grief to gratitude / Robert A.
Jonas.
        p.   cm.
    Includes bibliographical references.
    ISBN 0-8245-1552-8
    1. Bereavement—Psychological aspects.   2. Grief.   3. Infants
(Newborn)—Death—Psychological aspects.   4. Jonas, Robert A.
I. Title.
BF575.G7J65   1996
155.9'37'092—dc20   95-51043
                                                                      CIP

To Rebecca
(1992)
and to my grandfather, Fred Radenz
(1896–1995)

Contents

Acknowledgments

I thank my wife, Margaret Bullitt-Jonas, mother of Rebecca and Sam, for the Christ-light she brings into the world, and for all the laughter, love, and tears we have shared.

I give thanks to my daughter Christy, whose friendship, love, and sparkling conversations have often called me out into new life; and I bow in the direction of my sister Jolene and my brother Steve, whose total dedication to the loving responsibilities of parenthood are a continuing inspiration.

I bless and thank my brother-in-law John Bullitt, for his brotherly love, and for the example of such deep commitment to the spiritual arts of fathering and creativity. And I express my deepest gratitude to Margaret's mother, Sarah Doering, whose love, wisdom, and generosity of spirit and resources sustain so many.

Rebecca's story arises in the passage of life from one generation to another. I give thanks for those who gave me life, especially my mother, Virginia Senner, my father, Robert Jonas, my stepfather, Al Senner, and my grandparents, Leona and Fred Radenz, and Hazel and Leo Jonas. My deepest gratitude goes out to Beatrice Radenz and Eugene Radenz and their families for their tireless, loving care of Grandpa Radenz as he moves into his one-hundredth year of life.

Rebecca awakened me to the inestimable value of community. I give thanks to the men of my men's groups, and my friends Henri Nouwen, Eugene Smith, Kevin Hunt, and Paul Fohlin, all of whom sat with me regularly and lovingly during periods of intense grief. Through Henri, I have felt held by L'Arche and its vision of a Christ-centered community. Inspired by L'Arche, and in the shadow of grieving for Rebecca, the Empty Bell sanctuary was given to me as a holy place to offer spiritual healing and interfaith dialogue. I give thanks for all those who bring their joy and woundedness to that place. Their trust and hope inspire me each day and help me to find always new blessings in Rebecca's brief life.

Many friends have nurtured this book into being. Henri first suggested the idea that Rebecca's story should be told. Richard Payne, the editor-in-chief of the Classics of Western Spirituality series, worked lovingly and carefully with me in the early stages to help me find my voice. Dawn Gibeau, of the *National Catholic Reporter,* helped me to sculpt the shape of *Rebecca* out of a mountain of words. Several friends and relatives, including my wife, Margaret, Jeff Campbell, and Jim Lassen-Willems read early versions of *Rebecca* and gave invaluable feedback. For the theological thinking that is implicit in this book, I am in debt to my professors at the Weston Jesuit School of Theology, especially my advisor, Brian McDermott, a love-mystic and good friend. For introducing me to the Buddha and Dharma, I give thanks to Sarah Doering, John Bullitt, Larry Rosenberg, Joseph Goldstein, Barbara Rhodes, Mu Soeng, George Bowman, Jack Engler, David Duncavage, Connie Miller, Lama Migmar, and Lama Jorden. Their wisdom and guidance are tacitly present throughout this book. And I am forever grateful to the Crossroad editors, especially Bob Heller and Lynn Schmitt, for having faith in this story.

❧ Foreword

It fills me with much joy and gratitude to be invited by Robert Jonas to write the foreword to his book *Rebecca*. It is a long, beautiful, and still-deepening friendship that connects me with Jonas, as he likes to be called, and to this book.

I will never forget my first encounter with Jonas. In 1984 he approached me after a talk I gave at St. Paul's Catholic Church in Cambridge. He told me that he had been touched by my passionate love of Jesus. "You gave me permission," he said, "to be enthusiastic, excited, and even exuberant about the spiritual life." For Jonas, who was just finishing his doctoral work in education and psychology at Harvard University, that was something quite new and unusual. He wondered if I would be his spiritual director.

I still remember his radiant eyes, full of lively intelligence, kindness, and hope. Although I was flattered to be invited to be his spiritual director, I suggested that instead we meet as friends. I said, "I don't know who should direct whom, but I certainly would love to get to know you." This first enlightening meeting led to many more. We talked a lot, prayed often, shared many meals, celebrated the Eucharist together frequently and became intimate friends without any secrets from one another.

After this first year of friendship our lives radically changed. Jonas became engaged to Margaret. They married and had their son Samuel. I left Harvard where I had been teaching, joined L'Arche, a worldwide network of communities for people with mental disabilities, and moved first to France and from there to Canada.

During these years our friendship became broader and deeper. We visited each other in many places, and while I came to know his family, he came to know my community. Soon we began offering retreats and workshops together. While I spoke passionately about Jesus and his message, Jonas brought a dispassionate serenity and contemplative mood with his Japanese bamboo flute, the *shaku-hachi*. We found a way to model a good spiritual rhythm of fervent words and singing, and silent presence. We found ourselves in Providence, Rhode Island, Hartford, Connecticut, New York City and various places in the Toronto area, playing the "empty" flute and speaking the Word with much joy.

But then Rebecca was born, lived three hours and forty-four minutes, and died. Suddenly our friendship became a well of enormous grief. Suddenly our joy was penetrated by immense sorrow. Suddenly our long travels together brought us to a place of crucifixion. Suddenly our eyes so full of smiles and laughter were filled with tears. Suddenly our animated theological discussions fell away into silent, prayerful presence with one another.

Jonas and Margaret had been waiting full of expectation and hope for Rebecca. They so much wanted to have a second child; they so much desired a daughter; they so much hoped for a sister for Sam. Then one early morning they carried in their arms a tiny, lovely girl that could live for only a few hours—a little flash of light in the darkness, come and gone but leaving behind an indelible memory, sharp and painful, precious and beautiful. The three hours and forty-four minutes of Rebecca's life transformed all that Jonas and Margaret had lived before and would live thereafter. It was like the passing of God, splendid and terrifying.

As the weeks and months passed after Rebecca's death, Jonas could gradually ask himself: "Why was she here? Why was she given to us for a short while? Why did this happen to us?" As I listened to his questions I realized that they were not questions that came out of despair They were questions of vocation: "What is God calling me to?"

For many years Jonas had been a psychotherapist, teacher, and retreat leader. But he also wanted to be a writer. He loved poetry and always wondered if ever he would be able to share his deepest self in the written word. But it had remained a dream, a vague desire, an unrealistic aspiration. One day, as we sat together, talking about Rebecca, I said: "Maybe Rebecca came to invite you to write something simple. Not a dissertation, but rather a story, a story about her. It's as if you have seen an angel of God and you must write." Jonas knew immediately that I spoke the truth for him.

Other friends encouraged him, and so he began to write. Perhaps Rebecca had visited him to bring a new vocation—to speak with courageous vulnerability about the love of a grieving father.

Gradually Jonas started to see that his little, most fragile Rebecca, who was not even able to open her eyes, had been given to him and Margaret to give them a glimpse of God's grace. Gradually it dawned on him that Rebecca had come to reveal the mystery that the value of life is not dependent on the hours, days, or years it is lived, nor on the number of people it is connected to, nor on the impact it has on human history. He realized that the value of life is life itself and that the few hours of Rebecca's life were as worthy to be lived as the many hours of the lives of Beethoven, Chagall, Gandhi, and indeed Jesus.

A story had been given to Jonas to tell, and today, several years later, the story is told. It is Jonas's story. It is also Rebecca's story. It is a book about grief, but also about gratitude, about anger, but also about hope, about fear, but also about love, about loss, but also about gain, about powerlessness, but also about power, about time, but also about eternity. It is a book about hospital rooms, but also about the universe. It is a book about being human, but also about being divine.

As you read this book, you can choose to read it as a senseless attempt of a father trying desperately to give meaning to a meaningless human event: the death of a prematurely born baby. But you can also choose to read it as a witness to the mystery that through the power of the Holy Spirit, God in Christ is drawing all creation into God's transforming, eternal Presence.

If you make the second choice, this book can give birth within you to a hope beyond all hopes and a love beyond all loves.

I am so glad this book is here. It proclaims the mystery of life by weaving a tapestry of spiritual wisdom, integrating insights from psychotherapy and prayer, Christianity and Buddhism, medieval mysticism and contemporary spirituality. Rebecca is at the center. She is Jonas's teacher in it all.

This book has given both Margaret and Jonas a new parenthood, it has given me an invaluable knowledge of the gift of friendship in joy and sorrow, and it will give Sam, when he is old enough to read it, a sister he will never forget. But most of all it is a gift for those who will read it and be enabled by it to choose to live life, not as a curse but as a blessing.

HENRI J. M. NOUWEN

Introduction

This is the story of my daughter Rebecca and the gift of love she brought. Rebecca was born in the sixth month of pregnancy at one of the world's most sophisticated hospitals. In spite of heroic efforts by my wife, Margaret, and a highly skilled medical team, Rebecca lived only four short hours. But in those brief, precious moments she changed my life and the lives of many others who were close to our family.

I learned about Rebecca's conception in the late winter of 1992, when I had been depressed and feeling increasingly preoccupied with the fear of death. As a psychotherapist I worked closely with suffering and confused people each day, but I often doubted whether the hours I spent in intimate conversations had any impact on global problems. I wasn't sure I wanted to help bring another child into this violent and sorrowful world.

Rebecca's death would force me to face ultimate questions: Is life worth living? Is there really a personal God? How could God have let this happen? I had been a Christian all my life, and for years I also had practiced Buddhist meditation. Now, when the chips were down, I wondered, am I a Christian or a Buddhist? What is the meaning of life and death? Is there life after death? How can I survive the pain of losing a child? Who are my friends? Which of them can I trust for emotional support? If loving someone always ends in loss, what sense does it make to love? This book chronicles my spiritual and emotional struggle with these questions in the months before and after Rebecca's death.

Throughout the year of mourning, I kept a journal to track the path of grief's gale-force emotions, not only for my own learning but also for others. This book, based on that journal, is an archaeology of grief. I was especially mindful of my gender. What happens when we men allow ourselves to experience deep grief? Do we lose our masculinity if we surrender to grief? And other questions arose. What is the relationship between spirituality and emotion?

Between psychotherapeutic healing and emotion? How does my suffering relate to the suffering of others? In the few months following Rebecca's death, I considered my inner life to be a safe laboratory in which to explore these questions.

Family and friends helped me find myself and my spiritual path. One of the most important friends turned out to be a medieval Dominican friar, Meister Eckhart. The dialogues with him in the second half of the book and elsewhere are pivotal. With Eckhart, I was able to let the Christian, Buddhist, and psychotherapeutic voices in me wonder, argue, and seek consensus on the test of grief that I was undergoing.

Finally, I believe that my daughter's brief life and death made me a stronger, more loving, and empathic father, husband, therapist, and friend. After her cremation, Rebecca's presence disappeared into wind, trees, mountains, creatures, and people, just as her ashes rose and spread into the passing clouds. She taught me that I and all of us are much bigger than we think we are, and much closer to God. I will always thank her for the love she shared in her passing.

I was glad I kept a diary in 1992. Rebecca had come and gone, but I could examine and reflect on my journal, an intensely personal recording of her surprising arrival and her premature, gut-wrenching departure. Writing this book, based on excerpts from the journal, has been a way for me to recover my desire to live, and to say good-bye.

 The Pregnancy

The News

That late March day, the woods around our home north of Boston had been transformed into a breathtakingly beautiful, white cathedral. The snowfall that had begun two days earlier still drifted down through the evergreens. I had spent the morning with clients in my psychotherapy office beneath the garage. Now I walked upstairs for lunch. Our friend Lawrie Hurtt, an Episcopal priest colleague of my wife, was visiting. She and Marg talked excitedly in the kitchen where they assembled sandwiches for lunch. Marg playfully pushed a loaf of bread into my hands. "Here. Make yourself useful. I need to make a telephone call."

Lawrie and I talked as we stood at the counter putting the sandwiches together. I knew what the call was about. Last night Marg had said that her period was ten days late. She didn't believe she was pregnant but planned to check it out in the morning. Having visited a walk-in clinic a couple of hours before lunch, she was now calling for the results. Part of me listened intently to Marg's voice from the next room. Suddenly she exclaimed: "What? You're kidding!"

My heart sank. "Oh no," I whispered. Lawrie and I looked at each other with open mouths. Marg said a few more words to the nurse, hung up, and then walked into the kitchen, looking amazed. The nurse had told her, "Congratulations! Sam [our three-year-old] is going to have a brother or a sister." The three of us looked at each other in silent bewilderment.

Walking across the kitchen into the dining room, I opened the sliding glass door to an outdoor balcony. Marg and Lawrie stood at the dining room slider, watching me as I went out into the cold, put my palms together and pretended to jump off. We laughed together nervously. Then Marg and Lawrie turned back into the kitchen, talking quietly.

Sitting down at the dining room table, I felt sick to my stomach. I thought, "I can't handle this. How can I take on another child when I'm so physically tired and unsettled about my work? The canyon trip was a bust and I have no more tricks up my sleeve for getting out of this slump." Marg and Lawrie continued talking as I sat at the table with my face in my hands.

The Canyon

Six weeks earlier I had hopped on a plane at Boston's Logan airport, on my way to the Grand Canyon in Arizona. I wanted to reflect on my career as a psychotherapist. Was I doing the right work for me? But there was another, perhaps more important motive: I was depressed and preoccupied with fears of death. I found myself lingering over newspaper stories about violent accidents and murders, and felt troubled by numerous dreams of danger and death. Coincidentally, several of my clients were struggling with mortality in one way or another. Perhaps I was stuck in a mid-life, psychological slump; perhaps I was in a spiritual crisis. In any case, it seemed to me that a trip to the canyon was a good idea. Psychologically, it would be a needed escape, a refreshing time for reflection. Spiritually, I imagined it might be a pilgrimage: maybe God was waiting for me in the canyon.

On my first day at the South Rim I sat at the edge looking out, down, and all around for hours, trying to comprehend what I saw. Beneath gray, rolling clouds, the earth opened into huge valleys that had been cut by water and wind through numerous layers of limestone, shale, sandstone, and quartz. From top to bottom, the exposed sedimentary layers in the canyon walls revealed successively older chapters in the story of earth's geologic evolution. All the layers had been named and mapped, but even so, one sensed a vast power at work here, far beyond humanity's ability to control. Their exotic names—Toroweap Formation, Coconino Sandstone, Temple Butte Limestone, and Tapeats Sandstone—added to the striking sense of mystery. Their ages stretched from two hundred fifty million years to two billion years. As I looked down into the canyon, thoughts ricocheted randomly in my brain, as it tried desperately to connect my little life to something so Big. For the first couple of days I could not find a conceptual connection. Still, I trusted that the canyon was coming into me, making me larger.

Now, as I sat at the kitchen table in shock, I remembered what the canyon had taught me about fear. The real-life seminar began when I joined a group for an overnight mule trip to the canyon bottom. Snow fell as we prepared to leave. The leaders, two men and a woman, wore leather chaps and cowboy hats. They were young, perhaps in their late twenties. The skin stretched tightly across the bones of their angular and ruddy faces. I couldn't stop watching those serious countenances as they called each visitor to his or her mule and cinched up the saddles with powerful jerks of the leather straps. Saddling up, one of the trip leaders said, "If there's a slide because the rocks have soaked up the moisture and burst . . . well, that's just *one* of the many possible disasters that could happen on this trip. So if you want to turn around and do something else today, do it now." Several of us laughed nervously.

As we began our descent, the lead cowboy turned around in his saddle and shouted, "People complain about the mules. Don't worry if they walk close to the edge. We teach 'em to do that so you can have a good view." Turning in our saddles to see how the others were reacting to his joke, we all smiled under the naïve assumption that he was exaggerating the danger.

"This is a national park," I thought. "The trail must be paved." I was wrong. The path was three to six feet wide, a slippery slope of snow, red mud, and puddles. An hour or so later, after we had descended about one thousand feet, warm air ascending from the bottom turned the snow to rain. Dark, thick clouds and rolling fog moved through the valleys, thousands of feet below. Occasionally a shaft of sunlight burst upon a hidden, ancient chasm. Ahead and beneath us lay wilderness where almost nothing was planned or constructed by human hands.

The trip down in the rain was to take the better part of a day. Ten mules walked and occasionally slid down toward an unseen, black-rock river bottom. We were told to hold on tight, relax, and stay close to the mule ahead. We were supposed to kick our mules occasionally, to get them moving, but I resisted. Should I kick my mule, named Wags, to get him going, or should I try to stay on his good side? Which choice would ensure my survival?

Downward-moving mules and swaying human beings made their way along narrow, precarious paths carved out of towering rock walls. Sometimes the sun broke through where the trail disappeared into the distance beneath us. Then, from time to time, a huge fog, probably the size of Connecticut, would roll in. No one spoke. The only sounds were the clop, clop of hooves on stone and mud, the whoosh, whoosh, whoosh of mules breathing, and the swish, swish, swish of nylon trousers rubbing rhythmically against the saddles. We all looked into the valley below, so far down that people, trees, and house-size boulders appeared as dots on the vast landscape. I thought about death. The beauty only highlighted my melancholy reflections. I thought how incredibly beautiful it was, and how incredibly defended I must be. "I'm crazy," I thought. "I'm afraid of death so I come here, sliding downhill on a mule just inches away from a thousand foot drop!"

Motivated by fear, I became absorbed in strategies for keeping Wags on the trail. I desperately yanked the reins this way and that. To my consternation, Wags continued walking on the outside edge of the trail, just as the cowboy had said he would. Sometimes Wags was so close to the margin that when I looked down beyond my thighs, I saw no ground at all beneath us. As we descended into the canyon with sheer cliffs on our right, it seemed that Wags's left side was often out beyond the edge of the trail. Because I couldn't see his legs, I had to trust that his hooves hit like sure magnets onto the mineral-rich trail. Switchbacks were scary places where the path suddenly reversed to the opposite direction. If one forgot to turn, one stepped straight out into space that was tirelessly policed by gravity. Gravity had no preferences and no mercy. Everyone who crossed the line dropped. Only the narrow trail and the mules separated us from the Great Emptiness.

As we approached a switchback, Wags's head sometimes continued on over the edge while his feet stopped to negotiate the turn. Looking out into the looming abyss between his ears, I was terrified that the rest of Wags would follow his head. I rehearsed in my mind endless versions of what the pair of us would look like as we tipped over into the distance below. Would I go quietly or would I scream? Would I keep holding tight to the reins as we plummeted to our deaths? I remembered an airline pilot in Los Angeles a few years ago. He knew that he had lost control of his jet and was going down. As he dived straight into the earth he said into the radio, "Bye, Mom." Would I do that? Wags's heaving, rotating body interrupted my reveries. As I leaned into the switchback, Wags's legs and hooves turned underneath me just in time to bring his head back around to the trail.

After a few hours of self-torment, I realized my worrying was not effective. "Either he's going to go out into space with you on his back or he's not," I said to myself. This situation felt familiar. Riding Wags into the canyon wasn't so different from my everyday life, after all. Suddenly I realized I had always unconsciously assumed it was *thinking* that kept me alive. I had assumed that my ideas and theories actually held reality together, and that without them, life would have no meaning. I had hoped that my good thoughts even justified me in God's eyes, convincing him I was a nice guy who shouldn't have to die.

But here, thoughts seemed irrelevant. They lay over the reality of things, like the top layers of canyon rock, the Kaibab Limestone, now way up above us. The Kaibab was old, but not compared to the Vishnu Schist, the ancient, two-billion-year-old rock that lay undisturbed in the depths, like a primordial, unconscious fear. I had always assumed that the first layer of awareness, conscious thought, was everything. Now I saw that trying to control weighty matters of life and death with conscious thoughts was like trying to keep Wags on the trail with the reins.

After all my training in clinical psychology I should have known this long ago. Hadn't I introduced hundreds of people to the immense undiscovered, inner world of the unconscious? Didn't I quote Freud in my master's thesis in theology and psychotherapy? He said of modern Western people:

> You feel sure that you are informed of all that goes on in your mind if it is of any importance at all, because in that case, you believe, your consciousness gives you news of it. And if you have had no information of something in your mind you confidently assume it does not exist there. . . . You behave like

an absolute ruler who is content with the information supplied him by his highest officials and never goes among the people to hear their voice.[1]

My hands were frozen tightly around Wags's leather reins. "These straps are my thoughts," I told myself. "I fear letting go of conscious thought control as much as I fear letting go of Wags's reins. I think I'm controlling Wags, but he's going to do what he's going to do." Life and death will do what they are going to do!

For the first time since we had begun our descent I took a deep breath. Something entirely new had opened up in me. I relaxed into it and let it come, whatever it might be. As Wags continued clip-clopping downward I wondered, "Why can't I live this way all the time, surrendering control, letting go into my destiny?"

That night I wrote in my journal, "Thank God for that mule train today. It is the metaphor that fits my life: I'm always riding on a narrow ledge above a canyon, into a blinding snowstorm. I'm terrified most of the time. Rather than live right into the terror with my eyes open, I run from myself. I distract myself with worry and try to control the future with my thoughts. I want to be released from this psychological prison someday, but for now I can only repeat, 'Don't panic, don't turn back, and don't look down. Simply breathe from the belly, and trust.'"

Making Room for Another

Now the kitchen chair was the canyon edge. My breakfast turned over uneasily in my stomach and a ticklish sense of vertigo rose up my spine. A few minutes later Lawrie and Marg left the house to take Sam to the babysitter's. Left alone, I tried to think. What would be so bad about another child? Unfortunately, solid answers quickly sprang to mind. For one thing, Sam hadn't been sleeping well again. He had never been a good sleeper. What's more, I was moving into my late forties with a child already in college, and I doubted whether I could find the energy for another baby. In addition, my work schedule was beginning to pick up and I didn't want to be sidetracked. Wasn't it time to put more energy into my career?

Finally, I had been hoping to travel. I thought, "With two small kids, I'll never be able to get away until I'm well into my fifties!"

Looking out into the front yard, tears filled my eyes, causing tree trunks, branches, and snow to shimmer in the midday light. It seemed as if light radiated out from all the broken places in the woods. Was it a projection, or was nature communicating to me? I somehow felt assured of a graced light, shining through my broken places. Pressing an audio tape of Brahms's *Requiem* into the cassette player, I drank in the music.

When Marg and Lawrie returned, we sat at the kitchen table digesting the news. How could this pregnancy have happened? Marg and I agreed we had been ambivalent. Our on-again, off-again use of birth control was evidence of that. We had assumed the chances for another pregnancy were slight. Marg's mother took diethylstilbestrol (DES) when she was pregnant with Marg in the 1950s; ironically, it had been marketed then as a way to prevent miscarriages. Several years later, the medical industry discovered that daughters of mothers who took DES when pregnant had contracted abnormalities of the uterus and cervix. The damage to Marg and others like her included "incompetent cervix." The phrase was strewn through Marg's medical records. Because of her DES problems, Sam had been a complete miracle, arriving when we were on the brink of adoption. Could we rearrange our lives again for another baby? Marg was obviously pleased. I didn't know what to feel. My recent mid-life crisis, my desire to focus more on my work, my fear of burnout and exhaustion, and, above all, the fear of death combined to make me greet this surprise pregnancy with deep reservations.

And yet, as the weeks went on, I was surprised by joy several times. I had never thought of myself as the father of *three* children, but I began to imagine how wonderful that could be! "The main thing is we're in love," Marg and I told each other. "If you, Sam, and I pull together, we can do it."

Marg, ambushed by occasional spotting of blood, tried to hold back her enthusiasm but was basically ecstatic. We realized how much love we had to give. Slowly, our identity as a four-person family (Christy, my daughter by a first marriage, was now away at college), was shifting to include a fifth. Marg began negotiations for a pregnancy leave. We called agencies that might send someone to help us through a period of bedrest, expected because Marg had to be in bed for the last two months before Sam was born. We bought Sam a new bed and rearranged our bedrooms to create more space for another child. By mid-June Marg was into her second trimester and feeling great. She bought a stroller for two children.

A Question of Identity: Dreams, Mysteries, and Meanings

An important dream came upon me in the third month of pregnancy. I dreamed I was walking in the desert beside an old, wise man. In the midst of a gorgeous field of multicolored wildflowers, beneath snow-capped mountains, we stopped. Suddenly great swarms of bees surrounded us. I sprinted first in this direction and then in that. My mind focused on one thing: how to escape injury and death. At first my eyes darted about frantically, looking for a way out, but gradually their focus returned to the bees themselves. I was in awe of the bees, of the beautiful way they gathered and entwined themselves, by the thousands, around branches and plants. The teeming, buzzing, yellow-and-black masses were luminous, magical. It wasn't just that they were grace-filled but that they were communicating their grace to me! They were not merely biological objects but subjects too, in relation to me. When I exclaimed, "You are gorgeous," the message was received, disappearing into their buzzing beauty. I wanted to capture their perfection on film. But I realized immediately that my motive was greed and attachment. I wanted to possess that pleasure forever.

When I awoke, the feelings of fear, awe, and happiness and a new awareness of my attachment to happiness continued. I had the unnerving sense that a vast, unconscious world had made a permanent breach into consciousness. With this realization came the certainty that my conscious, rational mind could not, by itself, comprehend the meaning and significance of the new baby being formed and nourished inside of Marg. Once again, I was being invited to let go. Choosing another child still seemed totally unreasonable, but the larger Self counseled, "Yes, there is danger and you are afraid, but there are also precious gifts coming to you if you surrender to them."

Assuming that this larger Self exists in a spiritual dimension, I decided to put more effort into the meditations and prayers of the two traditions I knew best, Buddhist and Christian. Out of these traditions, East and West, a single integrated, spiritual orientation was slowly forming within me. The Christian contribution was expressed in my assumption that the Self is the home ground of God: God, not the ego, is the center of the Self. In this Christian cosmology, "I" was, most fundamentally, an "I-Thou." "I" could not be separated from the "Thou" of Mystery, who created me, loved me, and welcomed me, even in death. Could I accept this "I–Thou" that was the real "me?" The Buddhist contribution appeared in my willingness simply to stay with reality, with the "suchness" of things. Could I experience things just the way they are, without always hiding in fear or manipulating reality with my ideas, in a vain effort to take control of the uncontrollable? Marg had a bumper sticker from the 12-Step recovery program that said "One Day at a Time." To live each day fully and to surrender to the reality of the moment was a spiritual goal of both great traditions, and I repeated the phrase like a mantra throughout the early pregnancy.

The dream of the bees was a significant spiritual milestone. In surrendering, one could endure the terrors of transcendent beauty. From the Christian perspective, my little, fearful, greed-driven ego needed to die. Jesus had said that only when a grain of wheat falls into the earth and dies can it bear fruit (John 12:24). In the Buddhist world, Buddha's Four Noble Truths identified our attachments, desires, and cravings as the root cause of all suffering.[2] Could I let happiness, joy, sorrow, fear, and other emotions move through me freely, without clinging to them or hiding out in them? I wanted the freedom promised by Jesus and Buddha, but until now fear and ambivalence held me back from a full commitment to either path of liberation. With the dream came comfort and assurance that while the boundless unknown territory of life beneath everyday, pragmatic consciousness might be sometimes scary and painful, it was *ultimately* welcoming and safe. I was still afraid, but inching closer to the edge of real spiritual commitment.

In March I joined a committee at the Boston Theological Institute to help organize a Buddhist-Christian Society conference. I would bring together six or eight spiritual teachers from both traditions to lead meditation groups throughout the five-day, August conference. With the news of the pregnancy I had put off making phone calls necessary to the conference. But by May, as Marg passed through the first trimester, I felt a bit more comfortable with the idea that we would be a family of five. Optimistically, I began making calls for the conference.

I also recommitted myself to playing the flute. I had been taking lessons with the Japanese bamboo flute, the *shakuhachi,* for about a year. My teacher, David Duncavage, was a Trappist monk before he fell in love with a Japanese woman and the *shakuhachi.* He got married and continued living in Japan for five years, practicing *Sui-Zen* (blowing Zen) and learning to make the flutes himself. Now I depended more than ever on our weekly lessons. We sat facing each other, sitting on meditation cushions in traditional Zen teacher–student style. Our lessons always left me feeling more grounded and focused, less anxious. Increasingly, blowing into the flute provided a daily entry point into prayer and invited me into deeper levels of surrender.

In June I noticed a new ease in my playing. David had been telling me for six months I should relax my lips. It was difficult. He had to keep reminding me because there didn't seem to be a direct connection between my brain and my lips. The lips refused to carry out my direct orders! Either I wasn't aware of my lips at all or I was too much involved, thus over-controlling them. "Let go of your throat muscles. Blow from your belly and diaphragm, not from your upper chest and throat," he must have told me hundreds of times. I knew intellectually what to do, but I didn't know how *not* to control the breath with my brain and my body tension. For me the lines of control went from my brain, from the *concept* "Blow," directly to the overwrought muscles of my lips, throat, and upper chest. The problem seemed pervasive: in my everyday decisions, and with

Wags and the *shakuhachi,* my brain and my ego were in cahoots: they wanted to be in control.

Then one day as I blew into the flute, I suddenly realized my *cheeks* were tight. In eight months of daily practice I had never noticed these particular muscles. But now, as I relaxed them, a new, more resonant sound emerged. A relaxed belly, throat, and face allowed an occasional glimpse of notes and tones that seemed beautiful in themselves. The beauty came when I dispossessed myself of effort and result.

A few days later I noticed when my cheeks were tense, my thigh muscles were too. Body tension was associated with the self-consciousness of trying to meet some standard. Suddenly I saw that all the little tensions in my body were places of holding back, trying to stay in control. The brain and ego "I" wanted to call the shots. But when conceptual and muscular effort fell away, my whole being participated in blowing air through the flute. Still thinking that surrender meant losing something or giving something away, my mind became silent before the apparent contradiction that surrender could bring gain. Letting go wasn't passive giving up, but rather an active, effortless discipline of mindfulness. Letting go of personal power and control allowed another, nearly perfect power to emerge from within. Perhaps I could let go and trust the unknown future that our new baby would bring.

Welcoming Rebecca

In the second trimester Marg had a medical test that determined the baby would be a girl. We named her Rebecca. I wrote in my journal, "I'm still scared about Rebecca's coming. Even though I am tired and was sick a lot this past winter, I feel optimistic. Before the canyon it seemed being in a family of four was perfect. But now we are five and I love it. Our lives are graced, as if the rails have been greased, and everything good is rolling along through us without resistance—as long as I don't freak out and try to take the controls again!"

Rebecca was due on November 17. If things went as they did with Sam, Marg would be on bedrest beginning in September. In

July our schedules of work and childcare had been adjusted for the fall. I was looking forward to two public presentations. The Buddhist-Christian conference was coming up July 30, and in October I would lecture on the medieval mystic Meister Eckhart. I naturally gravitated to the concept of spiritual surrender in both projects.

July was a joyous month. Marg was beyond the morning sickness of the first trimester. Looking ten years younger and beautifully pregnant, she felt great. I loved hugging Marg and feeling Rebecca kicking simultaneously against her belly and mine. Rebecca was very active at certain times of the day. Sometimes, when Marg was lying on the couch or bed, I would lay my cheek on her belly and talk to Rebecca. "I hear you in there," I would say, "We're waiting for you. . . . You're going to get tickled a lot when you come out!" I took pictures of Marg's belly so we could show them to Rebecca when she was older.

At first Sam was disinterested in all this, perhaps because Marg and I didn't want to overemphasize our excitement about the new baby until we had passed through the dangerous early months of the pregnancy. But by mid-July he was asking about the concept of "sister" and wanting to put his little hand on Marg's belly too. We played at listening to Rebecca's heartbeat and trying to figure out where her head was. We explained to Sam that she would sleep in his old bedroom, in his old crib. In a way Rebecca had already arrived. My daughter Christy, Sam's and Rebecca's half-sister, was getting excited too. After all those years as an only child, now she would have two young siblings and her first sister. Marg and I felt very much in love, and I was proud to think of myself as the father of three children.

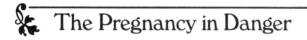

The Pregnancy in Danger

Bad News

On Monday, July 20, Sam and I accompanied Marg to Brigham and Women's Hospital for her biweekly checkup. Her obstetrician, Dr. Lichter, was on vacation, so we met Dr. Klapholz. He was in his mid-fifties, with many years of experience with DES daughters. Marg and I sat facing Dr. Klapholz's desk as he examined her file. Sam found a table with children's books and sat down to read. I asked if biweekly checkups were really necessary since Marg seemed to be doing so well. He agreed everything was probably fine, but said he wanted to be cautious, given the statistical dangers. "Just to be on the safe side," he said, looking at Marg over the top of his reading glasses, "I suggest you be very careful with your cervix. Let's not put anything up there. Unfortunately, that means no intercourse." Marg and I looked at each other in disbelief and shock. What? We had thought everything was going so well. Marg looked gorgeous, a healthy, pregnant woman. "Sure, I want to be safe," I thought, "but no sex? Isn't that a bit extreme? Maybe we can sneak in some rendezvous." I couldn't take him seriously.

When the doctor and nurse led Marg into the examining room, Sam and I tagged along. Sam was concerned about the blood pressure cuff. He asked, "Why Mommy sitting on table?" When the nurse found Marg's heartbeat and Sam saw it displayed on the monitor, he looked puzzled as he tried to understand "Rebecca's heart." When it was time for the internal exam Sam and I went back into the doctor's office.

Ten minutes later the doctor came out. When Marg came into the room, he looked up from his notes and told us everything was fine. There was just one odd thing, he said. The cervix looked good, but there seemed to be some cloudy material inside it. "Perhaps some mucus," he said. "It's probably nothing, but we should check it out more thoroughly." He told Marg she should come back the next day for an ultrasound and another checkup. When we left the room we were a little nervous, but we both sensed everything would be all right.

About noon the next day I took my messages between clients. Marg had called. She said I should come to the hospital. The ultrasound showed she was in labor! I called several clients to clear my time for a few hours and hopped in the car for the twenty-five-minute trip south into Boston. By the time I got to the hospital, the mild contractions had disappeared. A shot had stopped them when the cervix was one centimeter dilated. Marg smiled weakly as I walked into her hospital room.

I had found her at the high risk ante-natal unit of Beth Israel Hospital, hooked up to a fetal monitor and an IV bottle. We were surrounded by gurgling, blinking machines, green and amber liquid crystal screens and the quiet, regular thumping of heartbeats—Marg's and Rebecca's. "I couldn't even feel the contractions," she said as I slid a chair over next to her bed. "When they told me I was having contractions, I didn't believe it. But then I had to walk a block over to the labor and delivery building. I was numb, scared, and praying like crazy." Our hands reached for each other.

"It looks like the mucus Dr. Klapholz saw was actually the water sac beginning to come down. I'll probably need to be on bed rest until she's born, to keep pressure off the cervix." We looked at each other, unable to speak. In bed from July until October or November? It seemed impossible.

I asked Marg, "Do you think you might be able to come home? You could lie down there just as well as here."

"I don't know," she replied quietly, "the doctor will be around soon. We'll have to ask."

We started talking about Sam simultaneously. He and Marg had been so close. How would he handle it if she were living in the hospital for three months? At home, she could see him, read books to him, have dinner with him and say goodnight. When should we talk to him about Rebecca? How much should we tell him? Dr. Klapholz came by late in the afternoon. Indeed, Marg would have to be horizontal until it was safe for Rebecca to come out. She was now at the end of her twenty-third week. We learned the medical establishment doesn't consider an *in utero* baby viable until the twenty-fourth week. Chances of survival in the twenty-fourth week would go up to 5 or 10 percent. Could Marg come home? Dr. Klapholz said, "It's your decision, finally. Here at the hospital, we have the best machines and staff for an early delivery. But if she comes out now, there is not much we can do." I suddenly felt a huge hole open up in my belly. "We could lose Rebecca!"

Marg said, "We want to do everything we can to bring her out safely." I looked over at her. The muscles on her face were slack. I recognized her lack of expression as fear. Marg was looking intently at the doctor as we squeezed each other's hands. "It would be hard on Sam if I stayed in the hospital now, and it sounds like there's nothing to gain in being here." The doctor looked alternately down at his file and then at each of us in turn. "That's right."

"So let's go home," I said. Marg nodded. Dr. Klapholz interjected, "Just to be safe, I would like to keep you here one more day, to make sure you and the baby are stable. A little extra insurance that the contractions have passed." He looked at me. "You should be able to pick her up by noon tomorrow." He reminded Marg how difficult it might be to stay in bed when things needed doing around her. "But you must be firm about this, for the baby's sake."

I left Marg to pick up Sam from day care about 5 P.M. as usual. During the half-hour trip on Interstate 93 North, I reviewed in my mind all I would have to do alone if Marg were on bedrest for months. Clothes, food, day care, clients, evenings, mornings, bedtimes. Could I do it all without help? I would have to. "One day at a time," I whispered to myself. As we drove back south into Boston to see Marg, I told Sam that Mommy would be in the hospital for a few days so "Rebecca could get better." We stayed in her room about forty-five minutes. Sam was reluctant to sit on the hospital bed. He preferred a chair next to mine, against the wall, out of the way of the nurses. At one point, looking confused and concerned, he demanded, "Mommy! Put your clothes on. I want to go home."

Three weeks earlier we had bought a station wagon so Marg would have an easier time of transporting two lively kids. The next day, Thursday, July 23, I slid a mattress into the back of the car and drove south to Boston to pick up Marg from the hospital. When I arrived, I called upstairs from the lobby. Before long, a young man in a white coat pushed Marg down the hall in a wheelchair. We smiled at each other and hugged. "I love you," I said in her ear. "I love you too," she whispered. I had backed the station wagon up to a side entrance of Beth Israel Hospital. The three of us walked through the automatic doors into the warm summer air. The young man and I helped Marg onto the mattress. After gently closing the back door, I got in the car and slowly nosed into the busy, late-afternoon traffic.

Waiting for Rebecca at Home

When we arrived at home, Marg and I had tears in our eyes as we discussed where she would take up the vigil. We decided on the living room couch rather than our bedroom, so she could be more a part of daily life with me and Sam. I would set up a mattress in her office next to the living room where she would sleep. That night Marg wrote in her diary,

> A common project for the family now: to bring our fifth member into the world, healthy and fine. We each have a different role to play and burden to carry. I must be helpless and dependent, lying down all the time and unable to fix meals or clean up or play with Sam. Jonas must do all the housework and schlepping and childcare (with help from hired hands). Sam must bear the frustration of a mother who can no longer play.

Powerful feelings were awakening in me, but I was too busy to feel anything. Although Marg was often near tears or actually weeping, she wasn't melancholy or depressed. I admired her courage and her determination to make the best of a bad situation—returning home without her baby. And I was surprised and grateful that she could often smile and be incredibly creative in her play with Sam. She felt fortunate to have Sam to love, and he drank in her presence after the long hospital stays. From her nesting perch on the couch, she invented games to play and stories to tell. When Sam was at day care and when he slept, she talked with family and friends by phone, napped, wrote letters and read several books about preventing preterm birth. Marg was never comfortable with more than five hours of day care for Sam in one day. But now, because I usually had a full day of clients, Sam would often be gone for eight hours. This new requirement added to Marg's sorrow.

By Sunday the three of us had moved uneasily into the new routine of life centered on the living room couch. At first Sam didn't understand why Mom couldn't get up, but when he learned she could still read his favorite books to him, he brightened up. After a couple of days he stopped trying to drag her into games on the floor. The living room became everything—reading room, T.V. room, dining room, bedroom, and study. As Marg lay on the couch, we talked to Sam about Rebecca and let him feel her increasingly vigorous movements in Marg's belly. Sam and I revolved around her in the way people in northern climes huddle around a fireplace in the winter.

On Sunday one of Marg's fellow priests, Jim Diamond, came to give us Holy Communion. We pulled three chairs around the low wooden coffee table in front of the couch. Sam wanted to sit in my lap and watch as Jim brought out all the communion gear. Jim seemed adept at drawing Sam into the sacred activities. He gently invited him to take four wafers out of a plastic bag and to unscrew the lid on the small cruet of wine. When Jim started reading the liturgy, Sam, looking mystified, blurted out, "What you talking for?" "We're talking to God," explained Jim as we continued our prayers. Sam fell silent and watched with great interest. We all received the bread and wine, and prayed for our family, including Rebecca. Then Sam and I put our hands on Marg's belly as Jim anointed her forehead with blessed oil. I hoped and prayed Rebecca was taking in the healing love.

Marg Is Admitted to the Hospital

On Monday, July 27, I drove Sam to his day care in the late morning. Then I put the mattress into the back of our new station wagon and helped Marg walk slowly out of the house. We were on our way to see Dr. Lichter. He had just come back from vacation. I sat next to Marg in Dr. Lichter's cramped office as he reviewed the options. Now that we were moving into week twenty-four, the chances for Rebecca's survival were increasing slightly. Therefore it made sense that Marg should be admitted to Beth Israel. She would be close to the fine doctors and sophisticated technology of the new "preemie" unit. All morning I had fought back feelings of helplessness, rage, and sorrow, hoping for the best. I wanted Rebecca to be born safely, but I also wanted Marg to be home with me and Sam. We couldn't have both.

We discussed the option of Marg continuing to stay at home and being very careful. But Marg felt she couldn't forgive herself if she went home and labor started. What if we couldn't get to the incubators fast enough? Rebecca's safety was the first priority. Dr. Lichter concluded, "Let's admit you, just in case." Of course it was the right decision, but Marg and I were crestfallen. How would Sam take the news that his mother would be in the hospital for at least three months! I couldn't imagine running the house, taking care of Sam, doing my work and driving through Boston traffic every day.

For a moment, as Dr. Lichter and Marg talked, I almost fainted. Although feeling numb, I sensed an ocean of sorrow lapping against the office door. Emotions didn't seem appropriate here. The whole environment was cold and technological, inhuman, with charts that determined the day of conception and exam results on the computer. We talked about an *in utero* baby's lung development and the statistical picture of viability. All the while, a hidden part of me was pounding on the doctor's desk, demanding he save my wife and daughter! Marg was obviously worried. Dr. Lichter smiled and said "We'll get this baby out safely . . . you and me, kid."

I felt strange emotions in response to his words. I knew he meant to comfort Marg. She and I both needed to know he was an expert. We were putting her and Rebecca's life in his hands! But another part of me recoiled at Dr. Lichter's words. I noticed feelings I was almost too embarrassed to acknowledge to myself: I was uncomfortable with Dr. Lichter's intimate physical contact and emotional closeness with Marg. And I felt helpless because, it seemed, I had no important role to play. I was familiar with jealousy from other relationships in my life. But that this feeling would arise in a medical situation bothered me. It seemed inappropriate. What was the real issue?

At one of my men's group meetings, several husbands said they, too, had glimpsed such feelings but had let them go because of their obvious absurdity or irrelevance. Husbands are generally too busy with other things to think about their wives' relationships with their gynecologists. We are supposed to take the professionalism of medicine for granted, assuming that there is nothing personal about the doctor–patient relationship. One friend offered that we husbands are meant to see gynecologists as mere technicians. Especially in times of crisis, a body is just a physical thing that needs fixing. To a male gynecologist, a woman's body is just flesh, bones, muscle, and phlegm. Gynecology is one body after another, a job. This rational perspective soothed the male animal in us that responds emotionally when another man touches our wives' bodies. We husbands were uncomfortable with being too intimate with bodies—our own or anybody else's. If gynecological work must be done, we were glad someone was willing to do it.

Talking with these and other men friends, I realized that few of us know what our role should be during pregnancy and childbirth. A man's part in conception is clear, but after that, each of us is on his own. In the last twenty years, our mainstream American culture had liberated men from pacing back and forth on the outskirts of the maternity wards. When our daughter Christy was born at home in 1971, only a few hospitals in the world allowed men in delivery rooms. Today, almost all hospitals invite the husbands in. Times had changed, but most of us men still felt awkward in the intense emotional messiness of childbirth. Some of us learned how to do the Lamaze breathing with our wives' contractions, but few of us were given support in sorting out the complicated feelings that arose in the process. At home we made tough decisions in partnership with our wives. But often, in hospitals, other men took over. In relation to doctors I often felt self-conscious and irrelevant.

After Marg was admitted to Beth Israel, I drove north again to pick up Sam. As I helped him get his things together, he looked up at me with wide eyes and declared, "Mama's at home." He said it twice. Both times I distracted him. At last, when we were home, I explained Mama would be gone for a while but we would visit her almost every day. We called her before bedtime, but Sam didn't have much to say. During those days, he alternated between being obsessed with her absence and showing no interest at all. Just before bed that night he pointed at my stomach and said, "Baby boy in there." I explained only women grew babies inside their bellies. I said he and I couldn't grow babies. "Only mommies can do that." "Only mommies," he replied as he shook his head affirmatively. He seemed satisfied to have that story straight. I felt a new level of intimacy with Sam. He and I had a lot in common. Neither of us could have babies and we were both facing the loss of the most important woman in our lives.

Whenever I wasn't taking care of Sam, seeing clients, or visiting Marg, I was preparing for Friday's talk at the Buddhist-Christian conference. The title of my lecture was "Object Relations Psychotherapy: One Location for the Healing Work of Zazen and Christian Contemplative Prayer." It was a mouthful just to say the title, much less to plan such a broad, complicated lecture. On the Monday before the Friday conference, I was still uncertain about how to structure the presentation. Perhaps I would do a chalk-talk focused on the models of self or personhood in the three traditions of healing. I would try to speak from my direct experience rather than academically. All three traditions said that while we did not know our true, larger, and free Self, this Self could be discovered if we followed their path. Being excited about the complementarity of the three paths, I looked forward to presenting a synthetic model of healing, taking the best of all three traditions. But I needed time to prepare and I didn't have it. Stress was showing up in general irritability and outbursts of anger.

On Wednesday morning, July 29, I took Sam with me into Cambridge for my weekly *shakuhachi* lesson. He played with David's two children for the hour. Afterward we went on to Beth Israel. My mind worked overtime to remember all my obligations. Did I have Sam's diapers? A spare set of clothes for him? A client called in crisis last night. Did I get back to her? Was there food in the refrigerator? What school of Buddhism would I emphasize in my lecture, Mahayana or Theravada? Could I make some time to pray? Did I remember to bring the things Marg needed from home? Did I pay that Visa bill? Was Susan, our day care provider, set to receive Sam at odd hours this week? Did I remember to put gas in the car? I knew when my mind was so distracted, I might be prone to accidents. So I took special care when I drove. "One thing at a time," I counseled myself, over and over.

Around noon, after parking in the hospital garage, I grabbed Sam in one hand and two bags full of food, toys, books, and clothes in the other. Idling cars rolled in and out of the concrete bunker. There were real people in those cars, here for a reason. I could forget that. I wondered how they were doing, how they were coping with their diseases, pregnancies, and losses.

When we got to Marg's room, Sam cried out with joy and leaped up to her bed. After a lot of kisses and hugs we brought out his toys and he played on the bed. There was another patient in the room—a blond, pregnant, twenty-five-year-old woman. She and her boyfriend, the father of her soon-to-be-born child, talked quietly. Her name was Claire, his Richard. She was there for the same reason as Marg—her contractions had begun too soon. Now, after several weeks in bed, her baby was viable, and she was going home. The infant would have a good chance of surviving without the hospital's emergency machines. Marg and I shared pregnancy stories with Claire and Richard for a few minutes. Then we pulled the cloth divider around Marg's bed and held hands. Marg was worried. She had noticed a greenish fluid discharge that morning. The nurse said it was probably nothing, but she had taken a sample of it just an hour before. Dr. Lichter would come by soon to tell us what was going on. As Marg's anxiety rose, I became irritated with her. Some part of me knew this wasn't her fault, but I couldn't help myself. Thinking eventually things would be all right, I was angry that the pregnancy was taking up all my time and that I wouldn't be prepared for Friday's talk. Little did I know what was still ahead of us!

Rebecca's Birth and Death

The Waters Break

Dr. Lichter had always smiled and looked upbeat. I always felt reassured by his years of experience with DES pregnancies and his quiet, competent manner. But when he walked into Marg's hospital room about 1:30 that afternoon, he was not smiling. Yes, the waters had broken. The worst had happened. The protective water sac around Rebecca had ruptured. Green fluid was a sign the baby was distressed. We would have to act fast. I called Marg's brother, John Bullitt, and mother, Sarah Doering, to come to the hospital. John arrived about an hour later and took Sam home. He offered to stay with him during the crisis. Marg was taken to Brigham and Women's Hospital next door by ambulance. Sarah and I gathered her things and walked there to meet her.

The emergency ante-natal care unit was in the basement of Brigham and Women's. This took me a while to figure out. First Sarah and I got lost up on the third floor. It turned out to be my fault. I was supposed to be looking for the Ante-Natal Intensive Care Unit on floor L-1, in the basement. But when I had initially scanned the hospital directory, I had focused on the "Pre-Natal Clinic," on the third floor. Wishful thinking.

When we arrived at Marg's room, I was irritated and angry, but I couldn't figure out who to be angry *at*. "Why are these hospitals so impersonal?" I complained to Sarah. "Nothing but endless concrete corridors, and distracted, anxious people, fluorescent LED panels, digital readouts, and space-station beeps."

Marg's room was one of ten arrayed around a central nursing station. The low-ceilinged, circular room looked like recent construction. Well-lit and spotless walls, instruments, clocks, and chalkboards shone of white tile and paint, or stainless steel. Several nurses and doctors talked quietly behind the circular five-foot wall of the station. I could see women lying on beds in some of the rooms. Three unisex people, wearing gauze masks and white gowns, walked into and out of the area. A black couple in their sixties sat talking on plastic chairs against the curved wall, near a floor-to-ceiling stack of shelves overflowing with white gowns, towels, and sheets.

Marg was lying on a long hospital bed with a stainless steel frame. Pillows had been stuffed under her legs. Her gown was drawn up to expose her belly and a bed sheet covered her legs and hips. She looked tired, but managed a smile when we came in. One nurse was attaching a leather strap around her bare tummy. A sensor embedded in the belly-side of it was connected to a fetal heart-rate monitor which stood ominously on the other side of the bed. We could hear the whoosh-whoosh-whoosh of Marg's placental beat and the simultaneous tick-tick-tick-tick of Rebecca's heart. Somehow the same machine also kept track of Marg's mild contractions. A nurse watched the monitor and occasionally rearranged the strap so the machine could "hear" better.

The monitor face looked like a seismograph. A greenish sheet of paper rolled along slowly underneath a thin needle that reacted immediately to the whooshes and ticks of mother and daughter. As Sarah and I talked with Marg, I kept glancing at the seismograph, hoping if I watched it closely, both my wife and my daughter would stay alive.

Marg was being hooked up to the monitors by a nurse, when another nurse looked at her chart and asked us if our doctor had mentioned "Strep B." We looked at each other and shrugged. No one had mentioned it to us. She told us that in the preceding week, Marg had tested positive for vaginal Strep B. Technically, we were dealing with *Streptococcus agalactiae*, or GBS. Our nurse said perhaps the GBS had brought on Marg's contractions, but none of the medical staff had considered its presence to be significant at the time. Apparently, a large number of pregnant women (15-40 percent) carry GBS, and it is considered almost a normal part of the vaginal flora. But I noted the question in the back of my mind. Could all this have been prevented? It was a good question, but irrelevant at this moment.

A couple of doctors, a man and a woman, came and went. I can't remember what they said. I only knew it was very bad. With the waters broken, Rebecca would be unprotected from bacterial infections. She could not stay in there long. But if she came out now, early in the twenty-fourth week, her lungs most likely would not be developed enough for her to breathe. One doctor mentioned a drug that could be injected into Marg's bloodstream to hasten the development of Rebecca's lungs. But that would help only if Rebecca stayed inside for another week or so. Maybe the contractions would stop, allowing Rebecca to gestate a while longer. A small chance, but it was something.

As I spoke with the nurse about what the different sounds and graphic patterns meant, she paused and furrowed her brow. "It looks like the baby's heart rate is faltering occasionally. I'll call the doctor to check it out." A few minutes later a woman doctor with black hair, probably in her thirties, came swiftly into the room. Her name was Dr. Maria Maskola. Yes, she told us, this isn't good. The baby's heart rate was going down with some of the contractions. By now it was about 8:30 P.M. on Wednesday, July 29. Rebecca's heart rate was starting to go down with every contraction. The doctor explained the cord was being squeezed with each contraction. Our little girl wasn't getting enough oxygen.

Another woman doctor came into the room. Dr. Linda Heffner was tall, with light-brown hair. A gauze mask hung around her throat, as if she had just pulled it off her mouth. She must be the surgeon, I thought. As she watched the monitor to verify the problem, Dr. Maskola said, "Let's do an exam right now to see what's going on up there." She yanked some flesh-colored rubber gloves out of a box, pulled them on and then did an internal exam on Marg. It was necessary to determine where Rebecca's head and the umbilical cord might be in relation to the opening in the cervix.

My heart was racing as I held Marg's hand. Now there were two doctors and two nurses in the room. Everyone moved quickly and quietly. Dr. Maskola looked alternately at Marg and me and said calmly, "I can feel the baby's head. It's right here, but the cord is here, too. I'm trying to push the baby's head back." She brought both her legs up onto Marg's bed and knelt there, one hand inside Marg and one hand holding onto the bed railing. Dr. Heffner explained that Rebecca's head was coming down through the cervix, putting pressure on the umbilical cord. The cord was lying across the cervix. With each contraction Rebecca was being pushed down toward the cervix, thus cutting off her air supply. Her heart was feeling the strain. Dr. Maskola said, "I can't get the cord out of the way. I'll have to keep my fingers here, pushing the head up, so she continues to get some air."

That's when Dr. Heffner turned to Marg and me and said, "You'll have to decide on the dime, I'm afraid. You can either let nature take her course here, let the contractions do their work, or we can do a C-section and get the baby out of there right now. There are no guarantees either way. If we let things go like this, the baby will almost certainly not survive. If we get her out, there's a small chance, maybe 5 or 10 percent, she'll survive. I'm sorry we don't have more time for a decision like this." Marg, Sarah, and I looked at each other quickly. Dr. Heffner added, "If we take her out now, it will have to be an emergency C-section, which means a vertical cut from your pubic bone upward to your belly button, Margaret. We can usually be more cosmetic with a C-section. It's usually low and horizontal. But we don't have that luxury now. It will mean you won't have an option for a vaginal birth with future children. You'll have to have C-sections for all future births if we go ahead now."

I put my face to Marg's cheek and said "I love you" in her ear. "I love you, too," she said. I looked up at the doctor. "Is there any danger to Margaret with either of these options?" I asked. "No. A slight statistical chance of surgical complications like postop infections, but nothing life-threatening." I leaned over the bed so Marg and I could look into each other's eyes. Marg then turned to Dr. Heffner. "I don't want to die," she said. "Either way, you're not going to die," replied the doctor. Marg turned to me. "If the doctor says I'll be all right, I want to give Rebecca every chance." "Me, too," I said.

I looked back at Sarah. "What do you think?" She had heard us talking and nodded her agreement. She turned her palms upward, raised one eyebrow and pursed her lips. "If Margaret will be all right. . . ." I looked up at the doctors. "Let's go for it. Let's try to save Rebecca." Dr. Heffner looked at Marg. "O.K.?" she asked. "O.K." replied Marg with a slight smile.

Immediately the doctors gave the nurses instructions and began unhooking Marg from the monitor. Sarah and I stepped out of the way. Then the all-female medical team, two doctors and two nurses, began pushing Marg's bed out toward the operating room down the hall. As they slowly pushed her past me, I leaned over once more and kissed her on the cheek. "I love you," she said in my ear. I couldn't speak. Marg and her mother reached out for each other, squeezed hands and smiled. As they wheeled Marg's bed past the nursing station, Marg made a joke. I couldn't hear what she said, but I saw a nurse and a doctor laugh. With Dr. Maskola riding on the gurney, pushing against Rebecca's head so she could continue to get some oxygen, Marg, her bed, and all her attendants in white disappeared down the hall.

Rebecca's Fight for Life

Sarah and I stood watching Marg and her bed vanish around a corner. I was in shock. Everything had moved so quickly, I didn't have time to feel anything. I looked back into the empty hospital room. The monitor sat idle in the corner. Marg's bed was gone. Marg was gone! Before I knew it, I was weeping so hard I couldn't stop and had to sit down. My wife was lying on a table down the hall, naked. A bright light was shining down on her. Somebody I didn't know was going to cut open her belly and haul Rebecca out. Somebody else, a pediatrician, was going to take my daughter somewhere else to try to save her life. What if I lost both of them? Could I ever forgive myself for approving the operation? Overwhelmed with sorrow, helplessness, and fear, I was dimly aware that Sarah stood beside me. Her comforting hand rested on my shoulder.

I had never cried in Sarah's presence before, and I had never seen her cry, either. Though she was raised Episcopalian, Sarah's spiritual practice was primarily Buddhist. For ten years she had gone on many silent retreats in the Vipassana Buddhist tradition. I had also done retreats in this tradition and had learned a tremendous amount. My Vipassana teachers—Larry Rosenberg and Joseph Goldstein—had taught me how to climb down out of my head, out of my concepts and ideas about reality and into, or at least toward, reality. I learned to be quiet in the midst of pain and confusion, rather than to run away or distract myself. I learned to be curious about states of mind and emotion in a spirit of friendly investigation.

Vipassana offered a spirituality almost completely free of dogma, creeds, or other required beliefs. I appreciated the simplicity of the practice and its faith in the healing power of nonjudgmental awareness. And yet I often felt that Vipassana was a spirituality more suited to scientifically oriented people than to passionate, devotional types like me. In the Vipassana atmosphere, every emotion was to be noted, observed dispassionately, and allowed to disappear. One never considered that some thoughts and emotions might be inward manifestations of important relationships or graced windows into the Divine.[3] Sometimes, I came out of Vipassana retreats feeling like a cosmic newspaper reporter. Desire, passionate devotion, and loving attachment could easily be written off as spiritually inferior feelings. The Vipassana voice within me wondered if my fears for Margaret and my tears proved I wasn't detached enough, not perfect enough.

But I couldn't blame my reticence about emotional expression entirely on Vipassana. After all, I had been raised in a midwestern German Lutheran culture that required men to avoid all strong passions except anger. The feminist movement of the 1970s had inspired me to explore my more vulnerable feelings in relationships. Was the American version of Vipassana now reinforcing the outdated Western archetype of the passionless, invulnerable male?

Now, in spite of my reservations about her Vipassana practice, Sarah was simply there, and I felt safe. Fundamentally, I felt thankful for Sarah's gentle presence, and yet I also projected my Vipassana experience onto her: "Is she judging me for the outbreak of sorrow? Do my tears show that I am too attached to Marg or afraid of death?" Fortunately, the grief was too strong to be repressed by such judgments. I trusted that strong emotion did not indicate problematic attachments, but rather some truth and mystery about my relationships.

Sarah had always been kind and generous, so I let myself assume that she supported me and loved me, which I knew was the case. I wept because I might be losing two of the most important people in my life! And yet the self-conscious part of me needed permission to cry. That permission came when I remembered that the gift of tears is a recognizable, honored dimension of the Christian contemplative life. One weeps not out of sentimentalism, self-pity, or despair but because one has been broken in the presence of grace. In Christ, sorrow and joy are simultaneous events—painful but also liberating. The storm of grief soon passed.

A few minutes later I walked to a pay phone to call my daughter Christy, a senior at Brown University, in Rhode Island. I had doubts about calling her. It was raining outside. Was I asking too much for her to drive up at night in the rain? Christy and I had had some rough times recently. Was it appropriate to ask her for emotional support? Would she want to be here anyway, for her own reasons? I figured we could sort that out later; I asked her to come. There was hesitation in her voice, but she said yes. Feeling I desperately needed another member of my blood-family to be there, I was relieved.

Then Sarah and I walked through the basement corridors to the elevators. We zoomed up two floors to an Au Bon Pain restaurant near the main lobby. "Good pain?" I smiled wryly to myself as we walked in. I bought a frozen yogurt cone while Sarah chose a cup of soup. We were both exhausted and said little as we ate at a small round table. Looking into her eyes, I said, "I don't want Margaret to die." "Me either," she replied. Both of us were sad and scared. Aware of my mother and father's absence, I was gratified to have someone so caring from the older generation with me. Sarah and I decided to get back down to L-1. On the elevator I silently asked God to be with my wife and daughter.

At ten o'clock a nurse walked in. She said the operation was successful and that Marg and Rebecca were doing well. Marg would be in the recovery room for a while longer. The neonatologist, Dr. Simon Michael, had immediately taken Rebecca to a premature infant emergency care area and would come to see us as soon as she was stabilized. When he walked in 30 minutes later, I couldn't believe how young he looked. I realized with a start that most of the doctors were younger than me!

Dr. Michael spoke in soft tones. He explained his delay by saying he wanted to be sure Rebecca was getting the best possible chance. A small medical team had received her in the "preemie" intensive care unit. They were supporting her weak lungs by giving her oxygen "ventilation" and monitoring her blood oxygen levels closely. "The operation went well," he said, "Rebecca looked good when she came out. There was a bit of a delay in her breathing, but she got the hang of it and pinked right up. It's too soon to tell how things will go, but early indications are hopeful."

I was stunned that Rebecca might make it, but I also remembered she had only a 5 percent chance. The doctor said we could see her later. He would keep us informed. Sarah and I alternately paced the room and sat in chairs as we waited. We didn't talk much. The quiet comings and goings of medical people around the circular nursing station continued as before.

About a half hour later Dr. Michael walked in again. He said Rebecca had "lost some ground." Her little lungs were receiving oxygen directly from a tube that had been put down her throat, but they still were not keeping up with her body's need for oxygen. One danger with artificial ventilation was that a fragile baby's lungs could "pop." I didn't know what that meant, but it sounded horrible. "Unfortunately," he said, "that's exactly what happened a few minutes ago." Her left lung had "popped." She was going downhill and he couldn't tell us whether she would survive. He said, "We'll do everything we can to save her, but in the end it depends on her, whether she has the physical strength to pull through this crisis. We'll just have to wait and see what is in the cards for her." He turned to me and Sarah. "If you would like to see her, we could go now. Margaret will be in the recovery room a while longer." I was trembling as Sarah and I followed a male nurse down several hallways to the preemie intensive care unit. My daughter was alive somewhere in this concrete labyrinth!

Soon the narrow, low-ceilinged hallway opened out into a large open space with a much higher ceiling. Again there was a circular hub in the center, a nursing station. On all sides, rooms were arrayed like the spokes of a wheel. Intermittent low-volume beeps escaped from several rooms. Nurses and doctors in white smocks, a few wearing swatches of gauze over their mouths, appeared and disappeared from view. The place looked like a Star Trek movie set, humming with state-of-the-art technology. At the same time I was struck by the eerie silence. Everyone spoke in whispers. I could see incubators in several rooms, some empty and some with motionless tiny babies. The incubators with babies in them were hooked up to banks of silent, blinking lights. I saw no other parents and heard no cries.

Sarah and I washed our hands outside Rebecca's room and put on our white, sterilized gowns. The pediatrician came out to get us and we went in together. Rebecca lay naked on her back, spread-eagled on a white blanket beneath a hot white lamp. My first thought was what a shock it must be for her, to come from the darkness of her mother's womb into this bright light. A surge of anger coursed through my body. Rebecca's limbs were limp. An IV needle stuck out of her lower right leg and out of her left arm. Both her legs were black and blue and red, presumably from the doctor's efforts to find blood veins.

Her face was turned toward her left, and an oxygen tube was taped to her mouth. Her chest was heaving. The blinking red digital reading said "100 percent." Dr. Michael told us that even at 100 percent she wasn't becoming "saturated." I guessed she didn't have enough lung capacity yet to hold the oxygen they were giving her. I brought my face near hers as Sarah stood behind, a few feet away. "It's your daddy," I said as I stroked her forehead. Her eyes were closed tight. On her face I saw great pain, sorrow, and peace, all at once. A tall blond nurse stood on the other side of Rebecca, tending her. She asked if I wanted to baptize her. I was shocked at first. I said "Pardon?" She repeated her question, and I instinctively said yes. I never would have thought of it. I regret I don't know that nurse's name. She was an angel for me. A minute later she came back, holding out a small glass vial of water. I looked around and saw that Sarah had gone back out into the hall. The nurse retreated to another part of the room. I would be alone with my daughter.

Dipping my right thumb into the water, I brought it to Rebecca's little, wrinkled forehead. Brushing my thumb lightly over her soft skin, I made the sign of the cross. As I blessed her over and over with the water, I told her we loved her and that Christ and God loved her. "Father, Son, and Holy Spirit," I whispered as I touched her forehead again. "God bless you and keep you." For a second I wondered if perhaps I wasn't doing this right—was there some official phrase for baptism? I couldn't remember. I started to say the Our Father, but couldn't get through it—I wanted all my attention on her. I committed the details of her face and the feeling of her skin to memory. I wanted to get as much of her as I could in the short time I had. I whispered in her ear, "This is your daddy. I'm right here. I love you."

I wasn't ordained as a minister or priest. By what power could I do this? I found out later that this impromptu baptism was valid in most Christian traditions. But at the time I didn't know or care. I could only give her myself and what graces might come through me. My grandmother's face came to mind. She had died the previous year at age ninety-two. The daughter of a Wisconsin farmer, she had only a sixth-grade education, but she read her German Bible every night. My earliest memories included her bedside prayers, in English and German. "Now I lay me down to sleep, I pray the Lord my soul to keep. If I should die before I wake, I pray the Lord my soul to take." She taught me that Jesus is with us, whether we are awake or asleep, alive or dead. Later in life, even in the years when Jesus wasn't a part of my daily life, I would pray for my family and friends the way Grandma had taught me.

My surviving grandfather, Fred Radenz, was born in 1896. A housepainter all his life and a regular churchgoer, Grandpa was my connection to the pre-modern world. He never talked much about religion, but he drove across town to a German-speaking Lutheran church with Grandma every Sunday of his adult life. Now, as I baptized my daughter, I remembered Grandpa's solid presence the night my mother died of cancer. He had retreated from the family gathering, to be alone with God. As I touched Rebecca's forehead, I felt an everlasting love coming through me, from my grandparents and from their ancestors, to our daughter. Grandma and Grandpa were open windows into history for me. Through them, back through their parents and distant ancestors came the Light that created and loved us all. They, and that Infinite Light, were now present within me, ordaining me for this holy task.

Rebecca had almost no fat, so her body was very red, with blood vessels near the surface. She had a pug nose like Marg and me and a mouth with an upper lip like Sam's. Because she never opened her eyes, I had an eerie sense that she teetered on the brink of personhood. She was perhaps more intimately connected with the inner world of her mother's womb and with death than with us and our technological world. I could see Marg's, Sam's, Christy's, and my face in her face. Yet she was so "other," as if truly from another world. I stroked her forehead, as Marg liked me to stroke hers. Touching Rebecca's little hands and feet, I memorized the texture, color, and folds of translucent skin. My tears dripped onto her blanket. Making one last sign of the cross on her forehead, I blessed her again and then turned around and walked past several incubators and blinking monitors to the door. As I took off my smock, I realized Sarah had already gone back downstairs. I hurried along so I could be waiting for Marg when she came out of the recovery room.

About fifteen minutes later, at 11:30 P.M., Christy arrived, just as a nurse came to tell us we could meet Marg at Rebecca's bedside. The three of us walked down the hallways together, washed up, put on our gowns and waited for Marg to be wheeled in. As we walked in together, Dr. Michael approached us. I can't remember his exact words, but the message was that Rebecca was going to die. The nurses and the doctor who had been attending Rebecca brought in a six-foot high folding wooden screen to give us privacy from other babies and families. For the next forty-five minutes we hovered near her. We wanted to hold Rebecca, but it was difficult with all the tubes connecting her to machines and bottles. A doctor and nurse helped us to rearrange and disconnect a few tubes and wires. Every once in a while a beeping alarm startled us. I think it was coming from the machine that monitored her oxygen levels. Several times the nurse turned the beeping sound off and each time, after some silence, it would restart. The beeps and their accompanying, blinking red lights were meant to be warning signs. But now, silence surrounded these little explosions of sound and light. Our eyes were riveted on this quiet, tiny being struggling to live, and to die.

Now Rebecca was wrapped in a delicate cotton blanket. We brought Marg's gurney next to her, so Marg and I could hold her, one after another. We each spoke to her in whispers. At one point we both held her at the same time. Sarah and Christy stood nearby. I barely noticed Dr. Michael taking several Polaroid pictures of us during these precious minutes. Then as I held her, I asked him if there was any hope. He said they could keep her alive by machine for some time, but there would likely be great damage to her lungs or brain or both. Marg and I looked at each other, knowing this would be our last chance to see and touch her. I whispered in Rebecca's ear how much we loved her. The alarm bell went off again, and this time the nurse turned off the machine, it seemed, for good. The "100 percent" digital readout disappeared from the screen.

Rebecca's Death

Around midnight I asked Dr. Michael if I could be the one to take the oxygen tube out of Rebecca's throat. I'm not sure why I asked. Perhaps I ached for some way to participate directly in her life and death. Feeling helpless to save my daughter, perhaps I could help her die quickly, in peace. Marg asked the doctor about Rebecca's pain. He said she was sedated and so was not suffering. Slowly, lovingly, I peeled the white medical tape off of her mouth and pulled the tube out of her throat. Slowly, imperceptibly, her breathing quieted. Almost immediately she began turning gray. Rebecca died in our arms, on Thursday, July 30, at 12:07 A.M.

We held her a while longer. Dr. Michael said he would put together her belongings—the pictures, her knit cotton cap and her blanket—if we wanted. We agreed and thanked him. He said her body would be held there in the hospital until we decided about funeral arrangements. He would like to do an autopsy, but we didn't have to decide now. A few minutes later we were back in Marg's room. I would bring Sam later in the day, after we had some rest.

By the time I pulled into our driveway at 2 A.M., I felt exhausted, but the adrenaline was still pumping. No moon looked down in the black night. Like Vishnu Schist, the oldest rock at the bottom of the Grand Canyon, the night felt deep and compressed. Marg's brother John was staying with Sam. I tiptoed into Sam's room and listened for his breath. Hearing the regular whoosh-whoosh against the pillow, I felt my body relax. He was alive. A few minutes later John emerged from the T.V. room where he was sleeping. We met in the downstairs hallway. "How did it go?" he asked. "Marg's fine, but we lost Rebecca," I said wearily. He reached his arms out and hugged me, saying "Oh, Jonas, I'm so sorry."

I slept only a few hours that night. Determined to proceed with my life and work, I planned to go to the opening of the Buddhist-Christian conference in the morning. I was already awake when Sam got up as usual about six o'clock. I played with him for an hour and had breakfast with him and John. Then I called Marg. She had gotten little sleep, but she said she was doing O.K. "As the drugs wear off I'm beginning to feel the emotions. It's very hard," she reported. I promised to visit her after the opening conference session.

When I arrived at Boston University, I was gratified to see the large turnout: about three hundred people had signed on for the four days. It felt good to be out in public, participating in a larger world. I told some friends what had happened that morning and got a few hugs. Hearing of my loss, another staff person, Larry, said he would take over my job of coordinating the meditation sessions. Could I help him visualize the task? It felt good to be taken care of.

After working out the meditation schedule, I went into the big lecture hall for the opening ceremonies. The conference director, David Doepal, announced Rebecca's death and the death of a scholar who had been scheduled to give a lecture. There was a moment of silence. A few minutes later, my *shakuhachi* teacher, David, came out to play *honkyoku* (Japanese for "origin music"). When he finished, he said he would like to play an extra piece in honor of Rebecca. It was called *Ban-shiki,* or "Crossing Over." David was deep in his feelings as he played and the auditorium was completely silent to receive this gift. Some notes rushed through the bamboo so strongly, I thought the inside of his flute might explode. At other times the low, gentle notes felt like a soft caress.

Honkyoku are not played for the melody. It is ritual, liminal music, inviting one to experience each note fully as it appears and vanishes in the air. The gradual disappearance of each note brought the image of Rebecca's last breaths. As each one faded, some part of me cried out, "Don't go!"

Later in the day, I gave my lecture on spirituality and psychotherapy. About forty people came. The lecture went well and the dialogue that followed was interesting and fun. Several people said I had clarified many of their questions. Perhaps the lecture's clarity stemmed from my momentary, intimate familiarity with life, death, and God's presence. I put three circles on the chalkboard to symbolize the view of the self portrayed in relational psychotherapy, zazen, and Christian contemplation. Each view described the individual self as relational. This wasn't a mere academic observation for me. I simply could not conceive of myself apart from the people I loved, especially Rebecca. There would always be a "we" at the bottom of my "I."

Speaking as a Christian psychotherapist with Buddhist meditation experience, I emphasized the gifts each practice could offer the others. I made special note of my belief that the Trinity resonated at the heart of all reality. St. Augustine once said that, being made in the image of God, our true selves are transparent to the Trinity. In our souls we can find an eternal dance of Lover, Beloved, and the Love that flows between—a *perichoresis* (Greek for "dance around") of subjectivities. We may have opinions about who we are, and we may listen to what others say about us, but in our deepest selves we *are* a graced dance of God loving God. I had learned of Augustine's views in a theology class, but now I spoke from my heart. Who was I if I wasn't loving Rebecca with all my heart, mind, and soul? She and I were Lover, Beloved, and Love, and that was a glimpse of God.

After my talk I stopped in at a meeting of people interested in practices of zazen and Christian contemplative prayer. I told the group of fifty people what had happened the previous morning. It wasn't just the sorrow I wanted them to know about—it was also the love. I loved Rebecca, and even though she had died, I still loved her. And she loved me! Even though she had never emerged into full consciousness, I felt she was born to let me know that I, and everyone, was loved.

I explained to the group, "When I held her in my arms, I knew for certain she was a gift from God and that my role was to hand her back to God. A large part of me protested. I did not want to surrender her! I wanted her in my life! But I knew what I had to do." My sense that her brief appearance was purposeful seemed to transcend the human power of rationalization. "I can't say yet what that purpose is," I told the group. "I only know her birth and death have something to do with love, and that love's purposes are at the heart of this conference."

The Funeral Home: A Final Good-bye

Saturday morning, August 1, I got up early to pray. Today Rebecca would be cremated, and I wanted to hold her one final time. When Sam awoke, I ate breakfast with him and then called Marg, still in the hospital because of a postpartum infection. She was doing O.K., but her temperature hovered at about 101 degrees. Now I was concerned I might lose her, too!

At 9 A.M. I left Sam with Christy and my brother Steve. I began driving to the T.J. Conti Funeral Home in Georgetown. On the way I worried about our decision to approve the autopsy. We had agreed to it because we wanted to know whether the Strep B infection or Marg's DES problems had contributed to Rebecca's death. But I did not like the idea of some anonymous person cutting into my daughter's body. Her spirit and soul were with God, I told myself, and the information might be helpful. Still, because of the autopsy, her body would be mutilated. I wouldn't want to see her that way. I was angry at myself for agreeing to the procedure.

Marg and I had decided to have Rebecca's body cremated. Marg felt more strongly about it than I did. I wasn't sure. Was it disrespectful to burn a body? Was it a spiritual blasphemy? I had not thought much about it until now. I recoiled at the thought of anything about her being harmed anymore. Then two images came to mind: a documentary film of Gandhi's cremation and a Hollywood movie about a Native American tribe who put their dead up on high beds of branches and leaves, as an offering to the Great Spirit. If these holy people can choose to give their spent bodies directly back to nature, I thought, that would be good for my daughter too.

The funeral home director planned to cremate Rebecca's body at 11 A.M. As I drove east, then north, I played Fauré's *Requiem*. The sky was an eerie bluish gray. Out in front of me to the north, a bank of clouds lay low against the horizon. They shone fluorescent white above and dark gray beneath, rolling slowly away from me, toward the sea. Later, as I drove home in the opposite direction, I was surprised to see the same atmospheric landscape to the south. It felt right to me that the clouds were close to the ground, as if heaven and earth were bowing to meet and receive Rebecca. It may have been simply two weather fronts colliding on the horizons, but my heart said, "This is a cremation sky. It is wild, out of the ordinary and mournful. God is here."

Inside the funeral home, with its high ceiling and off-white, bare walls, a young man with black hair rose from a writing desk and introduced himself as T.J., the funeral director. Knowing I wanted to be alone with Rebecca, he said he had errands to run. He would be back in an hour.

T. J. led me to a large, carpeted parlor. Chairs ringed the room. I waited there with my flute, the Bible my grandmother had given me at my high school graduation twenty-five years ago, and the *Book of Common Prayer*. I waited for this man, a stranger, to bring me the body of my daughter. The house made no sound. I lingered by a window, listening to the silence. Then T.J. appeared in the doorway with Rebecca's little body, wrapped in a cotton blanket. She was so small! I wanted to take the blanket off, to see her again, but because of the autopsy, I feared what I would see. T.J. walked past me and I turned to follow.

He put another cotton blanket on top of a large wooden chest in the windowed alcove overlooking the driveway. A kneeler in front of the chest was the only religious symbol in the room. I thanked T.J. He nodded and walked out. In another minute I heard the screen door close as he left the house.

Suddenly I was stunned and immobilized by the silence. I would have felt the same way if Wags and I had slipped over the edge of the Grand Canyon trail. As if plunging in a silent freefall, whatever happened next would be beyond my control, at the mercy of the depths.

I stood in the middle of the floor looking at the small bundle on the chest. Here I was, alone with my dead daughter! Finally I took out my flute and walked up to her. Surrounding me was the presence of Marg and all the other family and friends who would have grown with Rebecca if she had lived. As the funeral home was on a quiet street, there were almost no sounds coming from the outside. The silence was both comforting and scary to me. If God or Rebecca stirred, I would hear. I listened. Rebecca's silence was more silent than a stone.

Breaking the eerie stillness, I walked up to Rebecca and started talking to her. I wanted her to know how much she was loved. She probably knew that by all the sounds and touches of love she had experienced while swimming inside of Marg. But I said these things out loud anyway, to declare them. "You have a wonderful mother.... God loves you so much ... but you're with God now.... Bless you, bless us.... God's blessing is coming through you.... Thank you.... I love you.... I'm so sorry I couldn't save you!" I thanked her for coming. Then I picked her up and slowly carried her around the room. She was light as a feather and the blankets were cold. I instinctively drew her close to my body, to warm her. Then I remembered she was dead.

Whispering to her, I walked around the perimeter of the room and imagined her whole life cycle. Diapers, late-night crying, being suckled, caressed, and tickled, grade school, boys, career, marriage, parenting, sickness, and death. Time and the boundary between life and death were irrelevant. I put her down and played two *honkyoku*—*Kyo Rei* ("Empty Bell") and *Cho shi* ("Tuning Heaven and Earth"). One note, called "U," could be played as a long mournful wail. The flute and I wailed over Rebecca's body. As the narrow stream of air broke audibly over the sharp edge of the flute, I saw her naked on the hospital table, trying to breathe. Other scenes, from newspapers and T.V. news came to mind, especially from Iraq, Bosnia, and Somalia, where so many children were dying and where mothers had cultural permission to wail and faint over the caskets of their dead. Fathers were not permitted such displays of grief in most cultures, but I was determined, and probably unable, to hold anything back.

Tears fell on the *shakuhachi* as it carried the breath and the music to Rebecca, beyond her to all those who were grieving, and to God. I wept for the love we could have shared in our wonderful family. Opening the Bible, I prayed Psalms 23 and 139: "The Lord is my Shepherd. . . . though I walk through the valley of the shadow of death. . . . You yourself created my inmost parts. You knit me together in my mother's womb." Touching the Bible to Rebecca's body brought her close to Jesus, to her great-grandmother and her unknown ancestors. Finally I read parts of the Rite II burial service from the *Book of Common Prayer*.

After an hour, I heard the back door open and close. T.J. had returned. Holding Rebecca's body close to my chest for the last time, I whispered good-bye to her and told her that I, her mother, and her brother and sister would see her one day. Then I left her on the wooden chest, knowing that within an hour she would be burned to ashes. The smoke from her burning body would rise into those shining white clouds rolling toward the ocean. "She's in God's hands," I thought. "But I wish she could be in mine!"

Driving home, I jotted down phrases for a memorial poem. A few weeks later, after more notes were added on my trips to and from the hospital, this final form emerged.

> *For Rebecca, from your Dad*
>
> Since you died, a storm always rumbles
> just beneath the surface
> of my chest. The world is
> more fragile, dangerous,
> and precious than I had ever imagined.
> I find myself suddenly, in a desert all alone,
> encircled by gathering clouds and lightning
> spreading out on every horizon. All around me is
> darkness and an extravagant, breathtaking
>
> > infinity.

Your mother risked
her life to save you and now dresses
the wound in her belly every morning.
Your belly was wounded too, and your limbs
were already motionless when
they brought me to you, your little chest rising
and falling hastily. Back and forth
from the hospital and then
from the funeral home I wept
and pounded the dashboard. Dammit! Dammit!

I feel empty now.
In my sorrow I reach out for everything
tenderly, as if I'm touching
your fragile skin.

Mostly I only know you by your absence,
a place in my dreams and memories
where you should be, but
are not.
Then suddenly I see you everywhere.

Yesterday on the freeway I was thinking
about my next appointment when
a bird flew into my vision and out of it. Tears
came to my eyes. A bow was drawn across
my heart—your bow. You are
every bird that flies across the sky. You are
every breeze that rushes through
or tousles the treetops. When I look
into the mirror I will see you,
as long as I live.

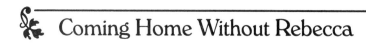

Coming Home Without Rebecca

An Emotional Roller Coaster

Marg finally came home ten days after Rebecca's death, almost three weeks after the crisis had begun. During that time I visited the hospital almost every day. Aware of stress, I tried to take one day at a time, and generally, I was able to be patient. Some days, especially when Sam hadn't slept well, lightning flashes of anger snapped through me. I could be irritable with Sam, Marg, Christy, or my friends and, with clenched jaws, I could drive too fast. On Monday and Tuesday, following the Buddhist-Christian conference, I felt numb, and I only realized the depth of my anger by noticing my behavior. I gunned the car around corners and was barely able to stop myself from throwing and breaking things. Luckily I didn't direct all this at Sam, though I'm sure he sensed it. Christy and I fell into disagreements and miscommunication.

Speeding in the car expressed a dark urge to destroy the world that had hurt me. More than once I fantasized driving into a tree or off a bridge. Sometimes the pain was so great I didn't want to go on living. I wanted to destroy myself, ending the misery. In that cataclysm, someone, perhaps God, would finally hear my cry for vengeance and mercy! But these suicidal impulses weren't merely destructive. Hidden deep within them stirred an almost unbearable love and an unconscious hope that I could meet Rebecca face-to-face. If I killed myself, I could be with her. Though I never gave notions of suicide any serious, prolonged consideration, their appearance was so shocking that a new level of compassion for myself arose. I wanted to become a better father, not only to Sam and Christy but also to myself.

Sam and I talked about his mommy every day and about Rebecca often. He would often ask, "Becca died?" And I would say, yes she did. "Why Becca died, Daddy?" he would ask. And I would say, because she came out too soon and wasn't ready to live. Actually, I thought she had been ready to live. She had been so lively inside Marg's womb, right up to the end. She had been ready, but her launching pad had fallen apart during the countdown. I wondered how much power technology really had and I recalled Dr. Michael, the pediatrician, saying that if she was "meant" to live, she would. "If it's in the cards," he had said, meaning technology couldn't help her unless she were strong enough to carry out her part of the effort. Few babies born so prematurely had lungs sufficiently developed to meet the demand. Still, I wondered if she had died because she lacked the will to live. I wondered the same about myself. Did I really want to live? Was it worth it? Maybe Rebecca inherited my doubts. I felt guilty, implicated in her death.

Another interpretation of Dr. Michael's "it's in the cards" was spiritual. Perhaps her death was predestined by God, a Calvinist concept that had once intrigued me. I was reminded of this idea when a young Asian woman at the Buddhist-Christian conference cheerily suggested Rebecca was meant to be reborn. But the more I considered these notions, the more depressed I became. If everything was foreordained by destiny or God, why do anything? My efforts to understand, to improve myself, to create something new, and to love and help others were irrelevant. Predestination presumed a distant God who set everything in motion, then sat back to watch it play out. Such a God was smug and perhaps malevolent.

I finally rejected this idea of God, preferring instead the notion that surprise was one of God's essential attributes, like omnipresence. Maybe even God didn't know how it would all turn out. I chose to believe God was intimately involved in our search for peace, love, and truth. Sure, since God was not confined to history, God saw all events at once. But wasn't it also true that God suffered, hoped, and delighted with us? I preferred to think that God too was sometimes astonished, saddened, or pleased by the course of events.

Every day Sam asked if Marg were coming home. Every day I didn't know. After the C-section, Marg's temperature fluctuated up and down for over a week. The specialists could not figure out what the problem was. The lack of information had me on pins and needles. Could I go on living if I lost her, too? Finally a doctor reopened the stitches in Marg's belly, cleaned out the wound and closed it again. A day later, her temperature came down to normal.

I was awed by her courage and her ability to radiate hope and love in the midst of such pain and danger.

On Friday, August 7, Marg's mother, Sarah, picked Marg up from the hospital, brought her home, and then left to pick up Marg's prescription for antibiotics. When Marg came into the kitchen we were alone together at home for the first time since she had gone into labor. We held each other and cried. After helping Marg get comfortable, I left to get Sam at day care. He was very excited, and jumped around in his car seat as Marg came out the front door to greet him. As they hugged and talked, Sam asked about the baby. He said, "She died." Marg replied, "Yes, that's right, Rebecca died, but Mommy and Daddy are fine." Back in our house together we were surrounded by Rebecca's absence. The house seemed deadly quiet just as if a fully developed person had died.

My emotions fluctuated wildly in the months after her death. I searched for meaning, rediscovering my prayer and meditation practices, and gobbling up spiritual books about death. Rebecca's loss reflected the human condition, full of promise but fraught with injustice. Sometimes an immense outpouring of love rushed through me, a love so great that "I" as an individual, disappeared into it. The angry protest that sometimes came through my fists was not just mine, but rather expressed a deep, timeless, great No!

Each week that went by brought new friends who had lost children. As Marg and I talked with and listened to other grieving parents, we felt an instant, intimate bond them, often telling our stories, crying together and hugging. Each parent's story was unique, but often the qualities of tender love and profound loss seemed infinite, transcendent of the individuals involved. I began to feel that "my" life was both uniquely mine and simultaneously not mine, a participation in a timeless story.

In my grief, I kept reviewing the events of the last months. I went back to Rebecca's conception in my mind. She must have been conceived just before I left for the Grand Canyon. How ironic that this new life began to grow just when I was obsessed with death. Or were my obsessions a premonition?

After the canyon trip, and after Marg and I had recovered from the shock of Rebecca's conception, we felt she was a surprising, wonderful gift from God. She was also the result of Marg's and my loving each other with our usual enthusiasm. I found it hard to reconcile my spiritual experience with this tragedy. Even though vaguely aware that my struggle for meaning was an attempt to ease the pain, the questions swirled through my frantic mind. Could there be something wrong with my love for Marg, and hers for me? Didn't we do everything right, according to the world's best wisdom? Didn't we love each other like crazy and let our love blossom into a family, making space for little ones to flourish? But if we did everything so right, why did things end up this way? Suddenly I realized the naïveté of my hidden assumption that love inevitably brings good things.

The dark, meandering intensity of my feelings after Rebecca's death seemed to peak periodically in anger and frustration. Because Marg was physically weak in August, I spent a good deal of the time doing house and family maintenance tasks. After Rebecca's death, mid-life career questions and self-doubts came back with a fury, but I had no time to address them. I hungered for opportunities to sit, write, and pray, but the household chores, Sam's needs, and the bills seemed to rain down endlessly upon me. Every day I saw Marg dressing the deep wound in her belly.

I loved being with Sam, helping Marg recover and working with my clients, yet it seemed I was always taking care of somebody. I recognized the old dysfunctional pattern of denial. I would put all my attention on other people's needs or the concrete requirements of daily life. When I lived like that, life was less painful, but it also became meaningless and joyless.

Years of meditation, prayer, psychotherapy, and a healthy marriage enabled me to recognize symptoms of denial and depression much sooner than in the past. I had trained myself to recognize certain clues to my state of mind and heart. Anger was one clue. As a child in an alcoholic, nominally Lutheran family, I had been taught that anger was bad. God didn't like it. But recently I had learned that irritation and anger could be more than letting off steam. Anger could be a sign that some important part of me had been abandoned, or that some real abuse or injustice needed attention. Aquinas had noted the complexity of anger in his *Summa*. According to him, some element of hope is always hidden in anger.[4] Sometimes, within the anger, I glimpsed the hope that my pain would be seen, appreciated, and taken away.

I also noticed a wildness in the anger, as it hunted for available targets. I was angry with Marg's mother for having taken DES in the 1950s and angry at the doctors who told her to take that damn death-drug. I was angry at the government and the medical establishment and the market system for allowing it to be distributed. The doctors had told Sarah that DES would save her daughter, and instead it killed her granddaughter! I could feel justified in having such anger, but it never felt truly satisfying or realistic.

Sometimes a compassionate voice arose in me saying, "Don't beat yourself up about being angry. Your feelings are telling you something. You're overwhelmed. You just lost a daughter and you don't know what to do with the pain. It's O.K." Still, I suspected that there were different qualities of anger within me. Some might indeed be O.K., but others weren't. How could one tell the difference? As a graduate student, I had been trained in the clinical art of psychoanalytic object relations. I always thought it should be called subject relations, as it highlighted the way in which our private, inner voices are like presences within us, having been internalized from previous, intimate relationships. This training, along with my experience in Buddhist meditation, had given me tools for stepping out of intense emotions and taking a bystander's role to my own experience. I could see and feel the emotion without being consumed by it. I could ask myself, "What is this feeling really about? Where did it come from? Who is it about? Whose is it? Is some action being called for?"

Now, years after the Vipassana training, I still remembered vividly Joseph Goldstein's instructions: "Moment-to-moment awareness—this is the great enterprise of becoming free. Sit in silence, breathing in and breathing out. Bring awareness to the continuous flow of thoughts, memories, future-thinking, sensations, and other sensory perceptions. Note them; let these objects of awareness be; let them go and come back to the breath."[5] The path to liberation from the ego—and therefore from suffering!—was to be present to this experiential flow without getting caught up in it: "Notice the desire for pleasant sensations, thoughts, and perceptions, and notice the aversion to pain; but simply sit right through it all with no preferences." I had experienced the wisdom of this teaching. And yet sometimes I could not discern if I was doing a valid Buddhist practice or merely distancing myself from my feelings. After all, I had received decades of formal schooling based on the principle that objective, dispassionate reason was the royal path to reality.

In Christian liturgies and in prayers, I heard myself say Rebecca was "with God." But the Buddhist teacher within me, and the voice of reason wanted to know, Was this my actual experience or merely an idea to make me feel good? The Jewish-Buddhist poet Stephen Mitchell's voice echoed in my mind. Having read his *Gospel According to Jesus,* I too wondered if the idea of something surviving after death was, like Jesus' resurrection, simply a "poignant whistling in the dark."[6]

Within a week of her return home, Marg made plans for death announcements, an open house, and a memorial service. I was impressed and envious of her ability to take charge of the mourning process. But I was also irritated that she kept bringing the subject

In loving memory
of
Rebecca Bullitt Jonas

born July 29, 1992, at 8:23 P.M.
weight: 1 lb. 8 oz.
died July 30, 1992, at 12:07 A.M.

All of us go down to the dust;
yet even at the grave we make
our song:
Alleluia, alleluia, alleluia

up. I wanted to forget what had happened. With mixed feelings I helped by doing a computer mock-up of the death notice, based on Marg's sketch. She and Sarah liked it, so we took it to a printer. By the end of August we had sent out eighty of these notices to family and friends.

God Is the Most Present Thing There Is

Gradually, I understood that my love for Rebecca was bringing me into contact with a spiritual depth that was so deeply human as to be universal and timeless. I sought situations that reminded me of this depth; in meditation and prayer, in conversations with friends, in Sunday liturgies at our Episcopal church, in my *sui-zen* practice, and in spiritual literature. Most of the reading revolved around Meister Eckhart, the mystic medieval friar. He understood the cosmic dimension of grief. Grief involved the soul, and, he said, "wherever God is, there is the soul, and wherever the soul is, there is God!"[7] In God and in the soul, our usual distinctions of "here and there," or "past-then and future-then" are irrelevant. It seemed to me that sometimes, in special graced moments, our perceptions and emotions arise out of that sacred *Now*.

As I loved Rebecca through death's door, I sometimes glimpsed an infinite, loving Presence that showed barely a ripple of recognition of the boundary between life and death. This Presence didn't seem to come and go like everything else in my life. Presence was infinitely steady, faithful, and reliable. Only my perceptions and ideas about that Presence changed. With Eckhart's support, I saw that that same Presence had emerged, moment to moment, in Jesus' life. After the Christian trinitarian story, he called this Presence "Sonship." But I was aware of a resonance in Buddhism and Hinduism too. A sacred, ageless light illuminated Gautama Buddha. And, in the Mahayana school of Buddhism, there are Buddha Presences, transcendent Buddhas within us. All beings are gifted with Buddha nature. When our taken-for-granted, everyday self experiences its own transparency, the "I" who then perceives, speaks, and acts is "someone" who has existed from "beginningless time."[8] This "I" is both one's "true self" and a mystery. In Hinduism, Krishna is the voice of the holy, eternal Presence. In the *Bha-gavad Gita* he says, "I am the beginning, the middle, and the end in creation.... In the alphabet I am A. I am time without end."[9]

In the depths of all the great world's religions lives this eternal, transpersonal, infinitely compassionate "I." In Genesis, God says "I AM who AM." In Judaism, this Ultimate Presence is so holy that we hesitate to give it a name. No image or concept is adequate, and each one of us is made in the image and likeness of the Mystery. Jesus declared, "Before Abraham was, I am." This was the Christian identity that transcended ordinary categories of time and space. For us, "the Risen Christ" and the Holy Spirit are one Presence of love, mercy, and forgiveness. In those moments when I felt most fully alive, most fully in touch with present reality, my every-day sense of time-bound identity seemed miniscule by comparison. I wondered, Could this be what Christian salvation means, to participate in God's time? I remembered the words of my theology mentor, Fr. Lucien Richard. When I suggested a difference between God's time and ours, he replied nonchalantly, "Of course. Time is a human invention." I was shocked. Still, I warmed to the idea that while Rebecca had indeed died, she also lived forever, in God's Presence. In Christ, the Divine doesn't obliterate historical time. He fulfills it.

How could one hold this contradiction of death-in-life and life-in-death? It helped to know that the Christian contemplative tradition offered a verb to describe the activity of conscious presence across the boundaries of life and death. They called it "participation." It was a word often used by Neoplatonic Christian mystics in the first centuries after Jesus' death. Each particular, holy love participates in the universal, timeless Love, every holy desire participates in Desire, every holy hope in Hope, every holy beauty in Beauty itself. These universal qualities of Divine Presence illuminate particular, history-bound experiences, from the inside out, gifting them with ultimate value.

Rebecca's life wasn't simply lost in the ocean of eternal Life. Her brief life retained its blessed particularity, while simultaneously participating in eternal Life. If we saw rightly, we would see that our hearts participate in God's eternal heart and that our brief historical presence participates in God's eternal time. Losing children is a graced invitation to let our time-bound, self-absorbed hearts and minds become stretched beyond their natural limits. We are lovingly stretched both toward God and toward others. Either these deaths harden us and invite cynicism, or we get bigger to accommodate them. The time-bound dimension of my love tried to keep Rebecca alive *for me* in *this* life, while the larger, timeless dimension set her free for God and others.

I gradually began to see that the larger Love in us confers free space around our loved ones so they can flower and die, unhindered by our narrow, self-oriented expectations and desires for them. Love seeks to protect and to liberate. But even when those we love do not become free and even when we cannot protect them, true love shares their destiny—free or imprisoned—through deep empathy. Such love willingly sacrifices personal survival. I saw it in Marg. She was willing to sit in bed for three months and then to put her body under the knife so Rebecca could live. Of course, Rebecca didn't live, and that fact also taught me a spiritual lesson. Participating in Love is not a cure-all or magic potion. Sometimes such participation only makes the heartbreak more poignant. Jesus participated fully in God's Love, but he died on the cross anyway. His participation didn't save his historical life, but it gave birth to an eternal life on a human scale.

Sometimes this loving presence within me lent a lightness of being and transformed all my perceptions. Right in the heart of grief shimmered *a field* of grace. I could stand in this field and look all around to see grace bringing new life everywhere. Or I could walk in the field and meet others, some of whom were also aware of the incredible miracle of life. Chance encounters with other grieving parents could bring us into the field. One day the *Boston Globe* reported the tragic death of a teenage hockey player in Quincy, Massachusetts: sixteen-year-old Matthew Messing had died suddenly of a heart attack after being "checked" by fellow hockey player Josh Wingate. Young Wingate reported his deep grief and guilt, and then thanked Dennis Messing, Matthew's father, for his understanding. The father had told Wingate "not to blame himself for what happened. Then he told Wingate he loved him."[10] Right there, in that moment, something eternal happened. I felt the story in my body as an epiphany and a glimpse into the

Incarnation. In such moments, grace illuminates ordinary human events and makes them divine. In such moments we *are* in the presence of the Risen Christ. Right now.

When we are touched by grace, deep sorrow, joy, and beauty intersect in true intimacy. Standing in grace, one might say "I love you" to people who, until that moment, were complete strangers. In our Christian tradition, the empty tomb and the cross symbolize the awe-full truth, that new life comes out of unimaginable loss. We all stand in the Christ-field, at the foot of the cross. In order to have this experience, we must go beyond the recitation of dogma. We must give ourselves to Love and allow ourselves to be touched, as Jesus was touched when they told him of Lazarus's death (John 11). If we don't feel the grief, then we aren't in the field, and we miss the grace. When we allow our particular grief to participate in God's Grief, then, surprisingly, the grief flows. In that flow, everything and everyone appear perfect—created and destined for wholeness and love, even in the pain of suffering and death.

But my grief also brought another round of severe self-questioning from the ego. Why didn't I protect my daughter from death? Why wasn't I handling all this with more equanimity? Guilt, hopelessness, and melancholy sometimes overwhelmed me.

In Eckhart I read:

> Do you want to know correctly if your suffering is your own or God's? You can tell it in this way: if you suffer for the love of yourself, in whatever way it be, this suffering hurts and is hard for you to bear. But if you suffer for the love of God and for God alone, that suffering does not hurt and is not hard to bear, for it is God who carries the burden.[11]

Eckhart's view comforted me, and I found myself repeating his words as I went about my work. The question appeared like a pebble, dropped into a lake, drifting ever more deeply into my soul. "Are You carrying this burden in me?" Once I thought I heard God answer, "Are you letting me carry it?"

Receiving a Call at the Health Club

One Saturday afternoon in August, as Sam and Marg napped, I went to a local health club. As I pedaled furiously on the stationary bicycle, lifted weights, and did sit-ups, I pondered Eckhart's question: Speaking to God, I asked, "Are You carrying this suffering in me?" Soon new questions emerged: Are You really there? Do You exist, or have I only imagined You, as a way to deal with the grief? An image of the Grand Canyon appeared. The only way I could explain its profound effect on me was that it had been *calling* me and that the divine You was somehow involved in the calling. My rational mind considered the idea utter nonsense, but it seemed as if the canyon, or some power within the canyon both knew about and cared for me. It was as if the canyon had *invited* me to be as big as it was. I could see the canyon objectively too, as if it were simply "dead" matter with a superficial layer of biological life. I was also comfortable with the idea that the canyon was indifferent to me. But it seemed like a holy indifference. It was as if it were a living being, giving its beauty away unreservedly and inviting us to do the same.

This sense of *call* contradicted my previous assumption that spirituality was based entirely on personal effort, with God as a great Benevolent Spectator. Intellectually, I remembered Luther's admonition that grace is more important than "works." But in fact, I placed a high value on my own efforts in spiritual practice. I behaved as if faithful meditation and prayer, by themselves, would bring liberation, salvation, and blessedness. But if Rebecca and the Grand Canyon were *calling* to me, then something beyond me was doing some work too, and I could respond. Living a spiritual life was a participation in an eternal call and response, God calling to God. I did not have to attract the attention of God, who would *then* call me. The divine call and response were not an if-then kind of thing, but something instantaneous and simultaneous. Something, Someone was already calling to me, beneath the level of my conscious beliefs and spiritual practices, from within nature, Rebecca, and other life situations. Perhaps the Grand Canyon was to me what the Ganges was to a Hindu, a place where heaven and earth meet. Such holy places are an invitation to let the meeting happen within oneself.

In the Genesis story (28:10ff.), Jacob lay his head on a stone and received the graced dream of a ladder to heaven. Then he sanctified the stone with oil and called that very place holy. I had a two-eyed view of the event. From a rational perspective, it was clear that stones did not have even the biological substratum for consciousness. On the other hand, I valued the "participation mystique" of ancient peoples. From a spiritual, poetic, or mythical perspective, did Jacob's stone somehow *participate* in God's granting of the vision? Didn't St. Paul say nature itself is *longing* to participate in spiritual liberation?[12] Perhaps suffering the loss of Rebecca "in God" meant trusting that all creation moved along with me in my grief, in a deep, empathic participation.

Here, I seemed to part ways with those Vipassana teachers who had said that all experience boils down to consciousness and objects of consciousness. Sometimes, when I sat silently in meditation with Vipassana teachers, I would get the sudden, mad impulse to jump up, grab them by the shoulders and shout, "I am here! I am not simply an object of your awareness!" I felt strongly that Vipassana spirituality had much to offer Westerners and Christians in particular. But sometimes its practices veered dangerously close to narcissism when it denied the possibility that so-called objects of our awareness—whether thoughts, rocks, body sensations, memories, or other people—lacked subjectivity, and thus any ultimate claim on our consciousness and souls. Was it crazy to imagine that people in comas, profoundly handicapped people, dead people, forests, rivers, and animals presented intentionalities, needs, and visions to us that enlightened and enlarged our souls? What if "objects" of awareness—other people, *in vitro* babies, canyons, whales, and trees—were communicating something to each other and to us? Did it really matter that Rebecca couldn't speak English? If we were all living within a vast intersubjective web of being, then authentic spirituality could not be simply a matter of adjusting our individual states of consciousness for maximum personal benefit, but rather required a deep listening and a response from the heart in each moment, one to another.

We, in the rational, individualistic West find it hard to see that perhaps our subjectivities are not our own, but also participations in the subjectivities that surround us. We would take more care with others and with nature if we believed so. Slowly, I was forming

the opinion that genuine spirituality must hold up the 3-D charac-
ter of otherness, the "refreshing tang" of otherness which invites
not only an *acceptance* of what seems other within us but also a
response in the deepest levels of our being.[13] Gradually, I formed
the opinion that in Christian spirituality, the goal of meditation and
prayer is not merely freedom, but freedom *to respond*. The central
discipline of Christian spirituality is this: Am I, in this moment,
with this person, in these events, free to respond in love?

For many years I had valued and practiced "letting go" in the Buddhist traditions of Vipassana and Zen. I had learned how to sit still
and find a center of spacious presence in the midst of wild fluctua-
tions of thought and feeling. In the 12-Step programs for Adult
Children of Alcoholics, I had learned the wisdom of the saying "Let
go and let God." And yet, in this moment at the health club, I didn't
want to let go of Rebecca. Here was one attachment I would not
break. If that was her or God's call, I would take my phone off the
hook. I wouldn't surrender Rebecca, even though Jesus himself
warned that all attachments must go.[14] Rebecca had been *taken*
from me, unjustly. And I was beginning to realize that this injustice
wouldn't be the last of it. Eventually, everything would be taken
from me—all my family, my mind and body, and finally even life
itself. I found this both terrifying and comforting. Terrifying because I loved life and wanted it to continue for me indefinitely, and
comforting because I longed to be in that place where love continues uninterruptedly, that place where Rebecca was. As I pedaled,
the aggression of an angry protest rushed through my legs into the
whirling pedals even as tears of joy dripped onto my lap.

After a half hour on the bicycle I sat down at a weight machine.
Reaching up, I grabbed the ends of an iron bar that was hooked to
one hundred pounds of steel ingots. Expelling the breath, I pulled
the bar down to the back of my neck. Then, breathing in from my
belly I let the bar go back up to its resting position above me. As I let
myself go into the surges of anger, I pulled the bar down again and
again, growling quietly with each repetition. It felt good to protest
death with a deep, primitive howl. Tears streamed down my
cheeks. Embarrassed at first, I gradually let go of self-consciousness
and continued to pull the bar down and let it up as if participating

in a passionate liturgical drama. Perhaps this too was the work of letting go, letting my anger grow larger, "in God."

Suddenly, the sensations in my chest grew more intense, calling for my attention. The image of a growing heart came to mind, as if it were stretching with the expanding pressure of suffering and love, seeking to connect with everything, everyone outside of me. I looked around the health club and saw the precipice in everyone's face. All of these fellow human beings were poised at the edge of a great depth, many of them afraid to look down. But what did I really know about any of them? My judgments about others fell away. I was only aware of our common, human vulnerability to life's disappointments and suffering. I felt gratitude to be a human being among other human beings, and I imagined with admiration how courageous each person must be to go on, each in his or her own way. And I imagined that each one was being called to become someone much larger, even infinite in love, beauty, insight, and compassion.

The precipice I saw in others was the ever-present drop-off between life and death. We all carried the great canyon in our hearts. I often looked down at that edge in fear, but I was now surprised to realize that when I faced into it, the fear disappeared. I saw that when we love others as they step across the precipice, our hearts transcend life and death, hope and hopelessness, what is visible and what is invisible. Again, Rebecca was my teacher. As she went over the boundary into death, I held her hand and part of me went with her. I loved her all the way across the line, and when I returned I wasn't the same person. She had communicated something to me, called me out of myself into something greater. Now the mystery of death in God circulated in my blood and body cells, a gift from Rebecca. This change was permanent, not dependent on my intellectual agreement.

The temptation to become bitter over this loss, and angry in some generic way at life or God, often swept through me. I could "pump iron" from a bitter, self-pitying place, or from God within me. I knew people who had gotten stuck in the bitter place. I could see their stolid faces and set jaws. Bitterness was their protest, their attempt at some control in this crazy, lonely, vast, unjust universe where they felt no essential connectedness. Remembering an image of baking bread in my grandmother's kitchen, the words of Jesus came to mind: "The kingdom of heaven is like leaven which a woman took and hid in three measures of flour, till it was all leavened" (Matthew 13:33). Perhaps grace was a holy yeast planted in our hearts even before we knew enough to cooperate or protest. Grieving was a part of God kneading that grace into us. Gradually, the grace would work itself into our muscles and bones so that when we fell into death's ovens, God would die with us and we would become leavened, transformed, and reborn as large as God. I took delight in learning that the Eastern Orthodox Church followed the ancient Christian dictum of St. Athanasius (296–373 C.E.), "God became human, so that humans could become divine."[15] It is up to each of us to let God become human in us. We are each meant to become a manifestation of God's grace in all that we feel, see, think, hear, touch, and *are*.

I saw that our love for those who have died calls us to stay awake and to reject completely the temptation of bitterness. Many Christians think all forms of anger are bad, but I was learning that anger does not equal bitterness. Anger can be explored for its Godward elements. Anger is an authentic human response to great loss, and it becomes something honorable, creative, and life-giving when the yeast of grace works within it. Instead of isolating ourselves in malignity and self-pity, we open to an aggressive, sorrowful, and infinitely loving Other in us who declares, "I protest this death too! I loved her too, and I will miss her too!" In Christ, our "I" is fundamentally a "we," a union with God who loves us so much that God seeks to take our place and to suffer with us. On the cross, Jesus cried out, "Why have you forsaken me?"[16] Like Job and Jonah before him, Jesus expressed rare prophetic courage in his direct questioning of God. Likewise, when we protest in our grief, it is not merely our own self-protective ego who protests. The divinity *within* also protests.

To acknowledge the Sacred within is humbling. One's ego portrays itself as the captain of its separate destiny, like an intrepid explorer, seeing things and naming them for the first time. Ego doesn't care for the idea that *my* hunger for love, *my* grief, and *my* thankfulness are not only mine but also God's in me. As our egos die into God, we see that our personal stories are transparent to an infinitely larger story within us. Suffering "in God" is allowing our small stories to be like icons, transmitting a Great Light.

Such thoughts at the health club left me a new person when I returned home. As I drove back I was joyous, singing all the way. But some part of me, the part that hates pain, seized on my good feelings to declare the grieving over. Yay! Except, I would soon learn that though the intensity of grieving would lessen over time, the wound in my soul would never heal completely.

The next afternoon, August 11, Marg and I found the courage to look at the pictures of Rebecca. Marg had looked at them in the days after the death, but I couldn't open myself to the pain of seeing her again. Our pediatrician had taken six pictures as we held Rebecca in her last minutes of life. For a few moments Marg and I sat together on the couch, looking at each photograph in turn. Mostly we were silent, though occasionally we spoke quietly to one another about her and about that night. It was hard to look, especially to see again how her skin color changed from pink to the ashen gray of death in less than an hour. Part of me thought I was being masochistic to look at the pictures, but another part knew this was a necessary part of the grieving. Her image and memory still lived in me and called to me. After thirty minutes or so, Marg and I quietly moved on to our separate workdays.

Rebecca's death taught me how little control we have over our destinies. Maybe here, at the frontier of what we can control, we instinctively turn to religion and spirituality. Not that spirituality is an escape or a palliative, but rather that its real power and illumination arise only when we find ourselves in the pain and intellectual darkness beyond the horizon of our own strength and understanding. Spiritual discipline involves listening for the "still, small voice" of God that calls through others, and from within each moment of our everyday experience.

A Memorial Service

On Sunday, August 17, we held a memorial service at Christ Church in Andover. Marg had been the curate there for three years.

She recalled the quiet, pastoral setting of the cemetery behind the church and wanted Rebecca to be remembered and buried there. The rector, Jim Diamond, provided a clear, protective agenda of liturgical events within which we could mourn. A small group of mourners met in a chapel off the main church. I began with a brief statement about Rebecca's coming and going. Her life was like the fleeting sound of a monastery bell, like the mournful notes, punctuated by silence, in the ancient *shakuhachi* piece called *Kyo-rei,* "Empty Bell." Raising the flute to my lips I blew each note of *Kyo-rei,* until the breath ran out. At each succeeding in-breath, the air rushed into my lungs like the sea swelling into a small harbor. In my heart I saw that for Rebecca, for me, and for everyone, one day the tide goes out and never returns.

During the shared homily I read the poem that had been composing and recomposing itself in me for the last several days. Marg's mother, Sarah; Marg's brother, John; and her stepmother, Sandra Bullitt, shared heart-felt words of grief and thankfulness. Marg's half-brother, David Bullitt, read "Dirge Without Music," a powerful, loving, protest-of-death poem by Edna St. Vincent Millay, and our friend Lawrie wept as she read St. Paul's hymn on love—"Nothing can separate us from the love of God, neither height nor depth...."[17]

Jim offered a short homily about letting this death be a sign of Christ's love. As I listened, I imagined the hundreds of funerals he must have attended as a priest. Through him, Rebecca was being received into the Body of Christ. A vision of Jesus' baptism came to mind, as if the Spirit were descending on Rebecca, saying "This is my beloved daughter, in whom I am well pleased. Welcome to the community of the Beloved." For an instant, I felt ashamed to acknowledge that, while I totally believed what Jim was saying, a small voice of doubt kept popping up. I thought, "Being a Christian is magical and foolish. Maybe we're all caught up in a collective psychosis. Dead is dead, period."

I played "Amazing Grace" on the flute (with many unintended squeaks and tortured notes) while Jim prepared the communion. During the service Jim did a laying-on of hands for healing and invited anyone to participate if they chose. Marg, our friend Ruth

Redington, and I knelt at the altar. Murmuring the words of blessing, Jim placed his palms on each of our heads in turn. He dipped his thumb in holy oil and marked our foreheads with the sign of the cross.

Before going outside to the cemetery, we all gathered at the back door. A babysitter, Chris Jesser, had been playing with Sam in the nursery during the funeral, and now she brought him upstairs to join us. Chris held Sam on her knee with one hand as she put on his coat with the other. I looked at Marg and whispered to her, "Should we have Sam come along?" "I don't know," she replied. In the middle of our quiet deliberation, Jim crouched down close to Sam and explained to him that we were about to bury Rebecca's ashes and that he shouldn't be frightened. Everyone watched in silence while Jim spoke to Sam about the burial. I felt uneasy with Jim's approach, wondering if he was projecting the idea of fear into Sam. Sam's eyes grew wider as he listened, looking expectantly at Jim's face, and then at Marg's and mine.

Then I realized that Jim was right. I wanted Sam to be there with us, in the dirt and ashes. Our small group of mourners walked outside into a light rain. Several people paired up to share an umbrella. Jim led the procession to the cemetery grounds beyond the church. Two days earlier, Marg and I had come here with a shovel to remove a one-foot-square patch of sod. I had loosened the soil underneath, blessed it, and then replaced the sod. That morning Sam and I had gone out into the woods behind our house for some dirt to add to Rebecca's ashes. Now, as I approached the burial site, I carried my *shakuhachi* and the small pail of our dirt.

Forming a small semi-circle on the grass, we stood in silence. Marg, Sam, and I stepped forward. Kneeling, I pulled the sod back and scooped out the square hole with a trowel. Sam knelt beside me. I poured a small pile of our dirt into the hole and spread it out to make a bed for the ashes. Then Marg and I opened the box of ashes. Marg knelt down beside me and Sam. All three of us held the box as we turned it over, pouring Rebecca's remains into the grave. Tiny bone fragments stuck out of the gray and white ashes. With my finger tips I mixed Rebecca's ashes with the dirt from our home and the dirt from the cemetery. Sam couldn't reach the bottom of the hole so I brought some ashes up to his fingers. I wanted him to touch Rebecca. None of us spoke. Sam wanted to reach down further to take part in the mixing, so I held him by one arm as he leaned into the hole. His hand and my hand blended together with the dirt and the ashes. Dirt–Rebecca's body–Sam's hand–my hand, all one. Sam's face looked serious, but not upset. He clearly wanted to be a part of whatever was going on. I couldn't tell how much of this he understood. Kneeling in the light rain, Marg and I both cried for a moment and blessed Rebecca. Then I added another layer of our home dirt, filled the hole with cemetery loam, and made the sign of the cross on the top of it all. Finally, I turned the sod patch back over the ground.

The grief called for something more. I dropped down alone on my knees before her burial place. Lifting my bare hands up, I suddenly brought my open palms down forcefully onto the wet grass. I pounded the sod over and over. Inside myself I cried out, "Goddamn it, Goddamn it. . . . God bless you, God bless you." I slapped the sod with both hands again and again. Rage and love poured out of my body, into my hands. "It's finished," my hands cried out. Then, with a deep sigh I reached for the *shakuhachi* and slowly placed it on top of the grave. Bowing my head I dedicated the flute, my music, and my life to Rebecca. "For you, for you," I repeated to myself. Sam and Marg were holding hands, standing silently next to me. Rising up, I brought the *shakuhachi* to my lips, to play *Choshi* ("Tuning Heaven and Earth") for Rebecca one more time. As the rain fell, everyone stood in silence. Each note was a call of mourning, not only for Rebecca but for all who love life and now must say good-bye. I felt more alone than I had ever imagined, and yet it was as if a great communion of grief-stricken parents–past, present, and future–surrounded us, crying our tears.

After the service the group gathered for an hour or so at our house. A Jewish friend called it "sitting Shiva." On the way back home, Marg said she felt relieved. I did too. The funeral had made it final. It ended our first stage of grieving.

Finding Spiritual Friends

Loneliness and the Search for Community

None of my blood relatives, except Sam, were at Rebecca's funeral service. No one from my family came to the "sitting Shiva" experience either. My mother had died of cancer thirteen years before. The day after Rebecca's death, I had called my dad in California, but I hadn't heard from him since. My brother, Steve, was on the road with a crucial contract commitment, and my sister, Jolene, was across the continent trying to keep up with her own work and family. My relationship with my older daughter, Christy, had become strained in the days after Rebecca's death. Rebecca's loss had triggered other, earlier deaths for both of us, especially that death called divorce. Her mother and I had divorced in 1983. I didn't feel comfortable calling Christy back and she didn't call me for a couple of months after the death. The tension in our relationship was hard to bear because I loved her and felt powerless to communicate that love to her. Rebecca's arrival and death had stirred up primitive, unpleasant emotions in both of us, and now an underlying fragility had been exposed. The hurt of Rebecca's loss burned in my belly and blood and triggered a surprising, primitive longing for genetic connectedness. I had never felt such a deep isolation.

In the end I was thankful Marg had arranged the memorial service and the house visitation that followed. My ambivalence about "sitting Shiva" disappeared as I let myself feel comforted by our friends and Marg's family. Neighbors dropped in to give us words of encouragement and a hug. My friends Larry Deloz, Skip Windsor, and Jim Lassen-Willems called several times and left reassuring messages on the answering machine. Many people, including my Zen teacher, George Bowman, and his wife, Trudy Goodman, sent cards of sympathy and compassion. The men in my men's group, David Killian, Andy Canale, Hubert Jessup, and Bob Ver Ecke, listened with love to my story of grief many times in the months after Rebecca's death. Her brief life was creating a space of intimate meeting and community support that felt new to me. Still, August was the loneliest month because there was a pain in me no one could touch.

Fortunately, the weekly *shakuhachi* lessons provided a regular occasion of good, friendly intimacy. I kept to our schedule as if my life depended on it. The commitment sent down roots to hold me in the emotional winds of grief. David, like all good music teachers, was not merely a trainer of musical technique. He was a master of soul music. I knew David practiced each day, as did his teacher, Kurahashi Sensei, and Kurahashi's teachers, back through hundreds of years of Japanese *shakuhachi* masters, all of us doing *Sui-Zen* (blowing Zen). The masters came to sit and to blow through the bamboo with their life's breath, no matter what. I, too, would sit, no matter what. When I played the *shakuhachi* by myself, I was not alone. I sat with countless others who blew through the bamboo, through their fears, passions, relationships, and deaths. David helped me to know a voice of friendly, inner guidance. The voice said, "Come to this place each day, pleasant or unpleasant, and you will receive peace and strength." In David's company I felt the absent-presence of many other wise practitioners of *Sui-Zen*, only some of whom were now alive.

Following a spiritual discipline, no matter what, did not feel completely new to me. Growing up in a working-class German Lutheran culture inculcated an exceptional orientation to hard work, duty, and loyalty to one's vows. My primary caretakers, often my maternal grandparents, modeled an absolute regularity of meals, work, hobbies, and relaxation. Even the barrooms my parents owned required an invariable time schedule of deliveries, bill payments, food and liquor deliveries, cleanups, and repairs. These things had to go on if the family was to survive. It didn't matter that my parents often came home drunk in the middle of the night. One must receive each day's customers with grace and sustenance, even when hung-over, irritable, and numb from the previous night's excesses. I learned early on an instinct for right behavior, even when great rivers of unfelt emotion swirled beneath the surface. Now, meditation practice became my form of disciplined hospitality, and in this curious way, a connection to my forebears.

One day I had lunch with another friend, a fellow therapist who had graduated with me from Harvard. I desperately needed people who could listen without judgment or advice, and Bob Goodman was such a person. He didn't say much. The phrase that stood out was, "Please consider us as members of your community. We're here for talking, visiting, telephone calls, anything you need." Nobody had ever said anything like that to me before—or, alternatively, I had never let myself acknowledge the need for such support from others before. In any case, I was deeply grateful. Other friends let us know that if we needed anything, they would be there. By the end of September, Marg and I had received at least eighty cards, several bouquets of flowers and numerous telephone calls. Many couples who had lost children of their own contacted us.

While all the support felt good, it was also painful. For one thing, I feared emotional dependence and found it much easier to give love than to receive it. And for another, the love of friends and caring strangers could never substitute for family bonds, broken by geography, emotional distress, divorce, and death.

Sister and Friend

My younger sister in Portland, Oregon, Jolene, had also lived through our parents' alcoholic confusions, absences, and rages, and their divorce. Her spirituality was never as explicit as mine, but she had suffered and her heart had grown larger as a result. Christy had telephoned Jolene the day after the death to say that Rebecca had looked peaceful at the end. When I talked with Jolene a few days later, I remembered with her how a similar peacefulness came over our mother after she died of cancer at age fifty-four, about thirteen years earlier.

Jolene also remembered the slight smile on Mom's face as she passed from coma to death. Then she offered, "Maybe Mom is holding Rebecca right now." It was the perfect thing to say. We cried together on the phone, three thousand miles apart, but side by side in our souls. Then Jolene added, "Maybe Mom is showing her how to play cards, and maybe Mom has quit smoking." My muscles tightened immediately. Jolene remembered our family's card playing as a social activity that knit us together. While that was often true, I remembered the living room card table as an adult-centered scene spilling over with whiskey and clouds of cigarette smoke. Card games brought our family together physically, but sometimes reinforced an emotional distance. I couldn't remember any time that a family member asked another how he or she was doing and really listened to the answer. Everyone seemed distracted inwardly, thinking about something else that was never really talked about.

I replied, "Well, I don't know that people play cards in heaven, but I do like the image of Mom holding Rebecca." Intellectually, I knew the idea of a heaven somewhere else was crude and naïve. Freud called it wish fulfillment, an escape from reality. But I was beginning to see heaven as a reality of the heart, not of the head or of geography. Heaven gradually formed within the currents and countercurrents of grace and grief. It was an invisible reality, a placeless place, shining out from within the visible world, making every event an epiphany, if we were open to see it. Jesus, and most Christians after him, liked to speak of heaven as both "already" and "not yet." Gradually, I was learning to live in that divine/human tension.

I had no trouble experiencing the paradoxical concurrence of suffering, the longing for God, and God's already perfect presence. Some weeks after my conversation with Jolene I had a dream in which Love came with me to one of those card games. The smoke, alcohol, and lack of intimacy still hung in the air, but now everyone was being forgiven and blessed. The card-playing scene looked exactly as before, but everyone was bathed in light. I awoke with joy and a sense that any remaining bitterness in me about my parents' lack of good parenting was completely gone. I saw that all the members of my extended family, no matter how wounded, carried the seed of divinity within them. Many of them were too broken to express it openly. But now I saw that Love had been there all along and would not allow any of us to fall into the darkness. Rebecca had accomplished a reconciliation of my family-in-me, one that many years of psychotherapy had failed to do.

After talking with Jolene, I remembered seeing my mother's scars from her three C-sections. She once told me the story of my own birth. She had been in labor, on and off, for a couple of days. Finally she became exhausted, and the doctors simultaneously discovered that my heart rate was dipping precipitously. So they cut her open and pulled me out. Now Marg had a scar in the same place. Why did I live and Rebecca die? Finding no intellectual answers, I considered such questions to be like Zen koans, challenging me to seek meaning at a different level. Questions about life and death and their meaning sometimes invite answers that cannot be articulated, but only lived.

I called Jolene for emotional support several times in August. One day I left a message. That night she returned my call from Tempe, Arizona, where she was working on a computer project. She was in Grand Canyon territory! I felt better immediately. In the past Jolene had not understood my attraction to the desert. I told her that for me it was a God-place. But, as recently as a couple of months earlier, she had responded, "O.K., but for me it's just a lot of nothing, and it's boring." Now, after listening to how I was doing, she said, "You would have loved what happened here last night. This hotel where I'm staying is built into a hillside, into a giant rock. I walked to the top of the rock during a storm. Out in front of me lay a huge valley, filled with flashes of lightning! It was just gorgeous, beyond words. I thought, 'This is God dancing!'" At the end of our conversation she added, "Maybe God was dancing because Rebecca is with Him now." She had said in words the song my heart was singing.

Priest and Friend

My priest-friend Henri Nouwen was in England when Rebecca died. About a week after her death I called him there. Listening silently to my story, he understood immediately and affirmed what my heart was telling me, that Rebecca was becoming a doorway to God for me. After our talk I could only remember a few of the phrases that touched me. "Let her have a name among you," he offered. "Your love for her has not been in vain. . . . Let your relationship with her continue. . . . Know there is a mystery here. Let yourself enter into the mystery this reality brings. . . . Somehow, if you can meet this tragedy in God, your wisdom will deepen." He said he loved me and thanked me for calling him so he could "share some of the pain with [me]."

I called Henri in England a couple more times around the time of the funeral. More than anyone else, he understood the transcendent dimension of my grief and offered spontaneous homilies about experiencing death "in Christ." Henri's phrase, "in Christ" and Meister Eckhart's "in God" each sank ever more deeply into my soul. God was at work in both the heavenly and the mundane dimensions of my grief. In one conversation, Henri offered, "I love you and want to live this a little with you. . . . If you can, trust that this experience is given to you as part of the Mystery of God, to live your life ever more deeply. . . . Enter into communion with God. You'll find Rebecca there. . . . Trust that there is a larger embrace where you, Marg, Sam, and Rebecca belong to God." Even though I could not fully acknowledge my hunger for spiritual companionship, Henri's words were soul-food. I was reminded of John's Gospel, where food is so often used as a metaphor for spiritual sustenance: "Do not work for the food that perishes, but for the food that endures for eternal life" (John 6:27). Henri was a generous farmer in God's field. The intimacy of compassion we shared was the ground I walked upon in the fall after Rebecca's death.

My Children, My Friends

Throughout August, Sam spoke about the baby dying almost every day. "Becca died," he would say. We assured him that although she died, Mommy and Daddy were all right. I looked for opportunities to get to know Sam better and I was enjoying our play together more than ever. One day the two of us went to visit friends who had a farm near the ocean. On a gorgeous, early fall day with fast-moving clouds and warm-cool winds blowing our hair and clothes, Sam and I went out into a hay field and sank into the grass. We lay there, looking up at the sky and watching bugs crawl on us. Twenty years earlier I had managed an organic vegetable

farm in Chesterfield, New Hampshire. There I rediscovered the
fine art of bug watching. The best time for it is just before haying,
when the tall, thick stands of grass are a deep, rich green. One
could disappear into a tiny realm of living things that prospered
anonymously, unnoticed by the cars buzzing by on the nearby country road.

A beautiful, magical world thrived down there, and I felt so grateful to discover it with Sam, as I had with Christy when she was his
age. Once Sam's eyes had adjusted to the smaller scale of life in the
grass, he became my guide. Did I see the rainbow on that dragon-
fly's wing? The purple, furry tops on the tall grasses? The red stripes
on the black bug? For the first time I glimpsed us as a father-son
team and felt a rush of intense pleasure. But along with the joy there
moved an undercurrent of fear that I would lose him. I watched my
little friend like a mother grizzly bear watches her cubs.

In September, six weeks after the death, the intensity of my grief
lessened a bit. Whenever I remembered Rebecca I wept, but the
crying spells became shorter and lighter. Many friends told me the
pain would always be there. That frightened me. Until then the sorrow had been so consuming that I yearned for a return to normalcy.
On the other hand I wasn't ready to say good-bye to her.

I felt as if my relationship with Rebecca was changing. This
didn't make sense to me intellectually. How could I call it a *relationship* if she was never fully conscious? How could something
that wasn't fully there in the first place change? Every once in a
while an acquaintance would speak the words of that inner voice.
One friend, perplexed by the depth of Marg's and my grief, asked,
"How could you be so affected when Rebecca was only six months
along?" Another friend wondered if I was simply projecting my
own wishes onto Rebecca. I told the latter friend that perhaps he
was right. And then I added, "On the other hand, maybe those
wishes come from God in the first place." My friends' questions
reminded me of my relationships with profoundly handicapped
people I had known. Sometimes they couldn't move their limbs or
talk. Sometimes there were no clear signs of an ability to communicate. And yet I always felt that I was in the company of a person,

someone with a hidden "I." I was drawn to Rebecca's "I," even if it was a nascent one.

Rebecca was a *someone* for me, a daughter and a friend, whether it made sense or not. I found emotional and spiritual comfort and meaning when I addressed her as "you," even as I acknowledged that her "I" had not fully emerged. When I allowed her to be in the center of my life, the whole of life made more sense around her, more sense than it had ever made. She was an inner spiritual compass, a way for me to know whether I was living fully and well. She showed me it was possible to love someone or something fully, even if the actual presence was as brief as a spring flower. It was easier to cherish life when Rebecca was alive within me.

This renewed love of life awakened the same anxiety that had driven me to the Grand Canyon. How could I enjoy life if death is just around the corner? After Rebecca's death, this anxious dread sometimes attached itself to body symptoms such as a scratchy throat. In September I realized that the roof of my mouth and my throat and sinuses had itched continuously since the death. These symptoms were new. A friend suggested allergies. But why would allergies arise now, suddenly at age forty-five? My parents had not had such problems. There was a bubble on the roof of my mouth that wouldn't go away. I began to think, "What if it's cancer?"

Memories fed the fear. Between the ages of nine and twelve, during my parent's separation and divorce, I had smoked cigarettes and drunk alcohol. I remembered being only ten years old, taking a shot of crème de menthe before walking to school. My parents and step-parents had been in the bar business from the time I was seven years old until I left for college. Drinking alcohol and smoking cigarettes for emotional comfort had been a normal part of my childhood culture. Surely those excesses were now catching up with me!

But as I pondered why I should be dead already, gratitude welled up in me. After all that self-abuse, I was still alive, in the midst of a loving family and rewarding work. I thought, "Even if I do have cancer, it's a miracle that I am not dead already. It's a miracle I found Marg, and then another miracle-on-miracle I have three wonderful children. It's a miracle Marg and I became pregnant at all with

Rebecca and that she developed enough for us to see her." I was astonished to be alive.

I counted myself lucky to be born into the educated baby-boom generation in America. Our cohort of men, intimately acquainted with the emerging consciousness of women, has sometimes resisted, but often responded to the vision of fathers spending more quality time with their children. As a child, my only experience of such fathers came through T.V. programs like *Father Knows Best, Lassie,* and the *Rifleman.* When I began my own adventures in child-rearing I was surprised to find that it was painful to spend time with my children. After years of therapy and self-reflection, I discovered that their eagerness to be seen and loved awakened the little boy in me who never did get his parent's— particularly his father's—undivided attention. To love my own children well was both a joy and a mourning.

Like a monastery bell, my children's cries in the night and their ubiquitous emotional needs had invited me to choose between love and selfish isolation. They had exposed ever deeper layers of self-centeredness, and simultaneously awakened ever deeper layers of love. Gradually, the archetype of protective father took root in me. Fathering Christy and Sam enfleshed a waking dream that had come to me in 1971, during Christy's birth. Christy's mother, Joanne, and I had decided to do the birth at home, with a doctor friend, Bill, in attendance. By the end of the long, exhausting labor, at the moment of Christy's birth, Joanne was naked and Bill and I were in our underwear. Christy's birth, accompanied by blood, mucus, tears, and laughter, had stripped away our civilized identities and triggered a primitive "participation mystique." In the dream-vision, I was a Native American brave, sitting naked and proud atop my horse. Holding a spear, we circled a campsite deep in the woods where my wife, attended by a midwife, gave birth. Each child awakened that archetypal warrior in me.

I used to want the longest possible life, no matter what. But now I could actually imagine throwing myself in front of a speeding car or truck to save my son and daughters. All three of my children had raised my consciousness about what good fatherhood is. We are meant to create good, safe boundaries within which our families can surrender to their true selves and to their creativity. No child can grow up as a free, self-confident, genuinely loving human being without feeling safe, seen, and loved.

For the philosopher Martin Heidegger, all genuine philosophy and religion start with the sense of awe that there is *something* rather than *nothing*. He got it right. Awe and gratefulness. My children have given me that. Rebecca's brief appearance brought me to the edge of meaninglessness and despair. But it also birthed awe. Not only Rebecca, but everyone and everything in creation appears briefly and then passes into the darkness. What are the odds any particular person, cloud, friend, or flower will appear in any given moment? A trillion, trillion to one! In September a generalized sense of tender-hearted thankfulness came alive in me whenever I thought about Rebecca or played with Sam. Rebecca let me know that new life could come out of death. I should trust that my friendship with her sister, Christy, would be renewed. In a certain, rationally indefensible way, Rebecca had become a dear, absent friend who knew me better than I knew myself.

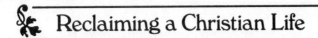 Reclaiming a Christian Life

Conversations with Meister Eckhart

On Time

The Eckhart lecture was coming up October 15. Throughout August and September I read his sermons with great anticipation. Fresh, surprising metaphors about the spiritual life abounded in his work and gave me a sense of hope:

> We are all meant to give birth to God.... We are mothers of God!... The eyes with which I see God are the eyes with which God sees me.

In my estimation, Eckhart is a spiritual genius. And yet, near the end of his life, in the 1320s, Eckhart was condemned by his peers and superiors in the church.[18] What a mistake! Rather than conveying the image of a wild heretic, Eckhart's German sermons impart a tangible sense of an ordinary person with extraordinary mystical gifts. In my grief, the intelligence, artistry, grace, humor, and loving-kindness of Eckhart's presence slowly coalesced as an inner voice with whom I was in dialogue. He was another absent friend, like Rebecca. In fearful moments of self-consciousness I was confounded by this "relationship."

"Look," an inner voice rebuked me, "this guy is dead and his theology is dated. Get off it." A Vipassana-like voice chimed in, "Your thoughts about him are simply thoughts. Let them pass." But my heart longed for Eckhart's words and presence, and I began to trust his brotherly advice. My usual notion of time—that the past is gone forever, and the future not yet here—seemed irrelevant.

Eckhart, too, walked a path of grief, singing his absolute assurances that no matter how bad we felt, God was near:

> No one may say at any time that he is apart from God, either because of his faults, or infirmities or anything else.... At all times, consider that God is near you, for great harm comes of feeling God is distant. Let a person go away or come back: God never leaves.[19]

According to Eckhart, when we participate in God's life, our ordinary sense of time is transcended. "Yes, Yes!" I blurted out as I digested his vision of a beyond that is entirely within. He wrote:

> I have already said often; there is a power in the mind which touches neither time nor flesh: it emanates from the spirit and remains in the spirit and is totally spiritual. . . . Indeed, the *now* in which God made the first person, and the *now* in which the last person is to perish, and the *now* in which I am speaking are all equal in God and are nothing but one sole and same *now*. . . .God dwells in a single *now* which is in all time and unceasingly new.[20]

Reading Eckhart was like talking with a good friend who immediately understands one's craziest thoughts. I was so excited to know that someone else felt the way I did about God's eternal Presence, but I wondered if we really did agree. For me, the emotions and my body were doorways to the infinite. Did Eckhart value human emotion? For me, grace often arose in the mix of some intense emotion and my longing for God. Often, in the rushing intensity of fear, grief, or joy, I stumbled into the field of grace. Then the world seemed as if it were absolutely new. For me, this sense of newness was an essential characteristic of grace. St. Paul once declared, "So if anyone is in Christ, there is a new creation: everything old has passed away; see, everything has become new" (2 Corinthians 5:17). And in Revelation (21:5), God says, "I am making all things new." Eckhart agreed with gusto! Once he declared that "only God's action is new," as if to say that God's action is the absolute standard of what "new" really is.[21] When we stand in God, we stand in Newness itself.

Gradually, the newness of *Now*, the availability of my emotions, and God's presence were becoming simultaneous within me. I noticed that intense emotion often signaled the proximity of some liminal territory where my usual conceptual labels for people, places, and events refused to stick anywhere. Everything became unknown and I became unknown to myself. Then I felt myself to be in the presence of a great, compassionate mystery. Perhaps this is what the Buddhists call *suchness*. Everything is what it is, everything stepping forward in its own particular beauty, connected to everything else in the living and dying flux of being. Rebecca and the grief of her loss brought me into such territory again and again.

I was learning that in the threshold moments, in the liminal ground between mundane existence and the Now-Presence, time is broken open. Rebecca lived and died *back there* in sequential time, but through the spiritual dimension of memory, she is always being born and dying *right now*. The same is true for my mother and great grandparents, their ancestors and all my descendants. It's true for everyone. Each of us lives in a timeless milieu of ancestors and descendants. In the heart's time, the *absence* of our mentors, families, and other loved ones is another form of their *presence*. In God, everyone and everything is present. Eckhart knew that experience, and I loved him for the courage to name and value it.

On Detachment: West and East

All my training in Eastern and Western paths of self-knowing came to focus on Meister Eckhart. I was learning to trust him as a Christ-bearer, but I struggled with his counsel about grief, not only for myself but also for all those clients and friends who sought my guidance. Did Eckhart see any sacred value in the unpleasantness of deep emotions? At first his advice struck me as confusing and unhelpful. He seemed to emphasize emotional distance rather than intimate, passionate living.

> If the spirit could attain formlessness, and be without all accidents, it would take on God's properties. . . . And those who have attained this complete detachment are so carried into eternity that no transient thing can move them. True detachment is nothing else than for the spirit to stand as immovable against whatever may chance to it of joy and sorrow, honor, shame and disgrace, as a mountain of lead stands before a little breath of wind. This immovable detachment brings a person into the greatest equality with God.[22]

Such quotes were a good example of why Japanese Zen writers assumed a kinship with Eckhart. They too seemed to identify emotional detachment as a spiritual practice and virtue. One venerable Zen Master, Dokyo Etan (1642–1721), said:

The one who practices meditation without interruption, even though he may be in a street teeming with violence and murder, even though he may enter a room filled with wailing and mourning . . . is not distracted or troubled by minutiae, but conscientiously fixes his mind on his koan, proceeds single-mindedly and does not lose ground.[23]

In fact, I had met Buddhist teachers for whom any emotion is an indication of primitive, unenlightened experience, or a sign that one is unwholesomely attached. I was interested in the philosophical similarities between East and West, but I most wanted *help* from these teachers, especially Eckhart. What did he actually *do* with his feelings? Did he feel emotional empathy?

Was Eckhart sitting back, criticizing me for causing my own suffering? Should I be a single-minded "mountain of lead"? Part of me was attracted to this idea. Being emotionally detached wouldn't hurt so much. But how was this detachment different from our Western "Marlboro man," who was merely out of touch with his feelings? How was Eckhart's detachment different from the worldview of the Stoics or the ancient Gnostics, who located spiritual life completely in the intellect? Did his detachment indicate hatred of the body and intimacy? Should I allow myself to miss Rebecca and cry, or should I try to transcend the feelings through meditation, prayer, and work?

Eckhart's voice seemed to counsel, "Remain detached from your feelings." But the late-twentieth-century psychotherapist in me retorted, "Detachment is isolating—a suppression and denial of emotion and the connectedness it brings. Feel your grief fully now. It will resolve itself in wellness and deeper levels of intimacy." The pastoral counselor in me chimed in, "Yes. There's something divine in your suffering. Eckhart himself said that we are all meant to give birth to God. Do you think that is a calm, emotionally detached process? You have seen a woman in labor. It's painful, hard work and it requires incredible concentration. Your emotional and spiritual distress are like contractions. Let yourself go into the waves of feeling and wait for the birth. Don't try to control the process. Let the contractions do the work." Whom should I believe? Out of sheer respect for his genius, I wanted to believe Eckhart. But his voice seemed to echo many early Christian mystics such as Evagrius (345–399 C.E.), who counseled that passions are a sickness of the soul.[24]

I contrasted the ancient Christian and Buddhist teachings of emotional "immovability" with my firsthand training in zazen. Zen Master George Bowman had taught me not to reject feelings but to become more intimate with them, even the unpleasant ones. As if my awareness were a mirror, I was to reflect the emotion perfectly, not to add anything to it and not to escape into a mere concept of it. I must match it one for one, to become it. If there is grief, then *be* grief, completely. When I could do this, I sometimes felt complete clarity and peace. But Eckhart and Bowman seemed to contradict each other. Should I ignore my feelings, step aside from them, look at them, mirror them, transcend them, analyze them, feel them, or be them? I was confused.

One thing seemed clear: Grief was teaching me that deep feeling is simultaneously personal and universal. When I surrendered into the feeling completely, as George Bowman suggested, I often found others. The depths of my personal grief always opened into the presence of others who were grieving, and finally into Grief itself. Sometimes it seemed as if there was only one Grief. I wondered, How is it that emotions can be entirely private, and yet connect us so intimately to *all* others and to creation as a whole? Was this insight a Christian addition to my Buddhist meditations? I soon realized that finding something universal in one's own experience is indeed a valid and valued insight in Zen.

In the Zen enlightenment experience one finds the universe within oneself, thus becoming what Zen Master Akizuki Ryomin calls the "transindividual individual."[25] Moving in a stream of ever-fresh awareness and total presence, all separation between self and others is overcome.[26] The suffering and joy of others become our own. I began to understand that Buddhist "detachment" does not necessarily indicate a lack of emotional experience. In fact, the emphasis is on being entirely awake in every experience, and *being* every emotion fully. The goal is to let down all inner barriers to our direct experience, surrendering to our emotions—and to the emotions of others too—more deeply. Detachment means that our ego is no longer the center of things, controlling things for its defensive purposes. I was learning that Zen detachment meant going exactly where the grief took me, no more, no less. The principle I carried within me from Zen was this: "Just this. Don't add anything."

With the help of Buddhist mentors I had glimpsed insight into "emptiness" (*shunyata*) and had seen for myself that all things, including my self, are composite. This insight helped me to have more patience with the many voices that seemed to be calling for attention within me. I was realizing that Buddhist detachment is an insight into how one's personal "I" is not a fixed thing or place within oneself but rather something dynamic and mysterious. If we sit still long enough, we soon see that our selves are composed of not-self elements—memories, the voices of our parents and mentors, cultural myths, personal plans, fears, inclinations, habits, and recurring and surprisingly new thoughts and feelings. Sometimes we can glimpse the truth of Walt Whitman's poetic insight:

> Do I contradict myself?
> Very well then, I contradict myself,
> (I am large, I contain multitudes.)[27]

We, in our very selves, are not any one thing, but many. One's self is a vast reservoir of complex and paradoxical emotions, all of which link us in intimate ways to others. For Zen practitioners, enlightenment is the direct realization of this inward, interrelated "emptiness."

Some of my Christian friends thought that Buddhism counseled a "negative" or nihilistic attitude toward the world. In fact, this opinion came to the surface most dramatically in 1994, as I was writing this book, when Pope John Paul II dismissed Buddhism as essentially opposed to Christianity. He wrote that Buddhism teaches that the world is "bad" and that enlightenment is a matter of becoming "indifferent" to the world.[28] The pope's opinion left me sad and angry, for my experience of Buddhist meditation and of Buddhist teachers is very different. For most of them, insight into "emptiness" is a kind of fullness, a fullness that comes from allowing the world to be just what it is. From my Tibetan Buddhist friends in particular, I had learned that compassion is one face of emptiness. In the light of Buddhist wisdom, one sees that "all human beings are intimately related, and one's own self and the selves of others are bound inseparably to one another."[29] My Tibetan friends had taught me the *Tonglen* practice of giving and receiving, in which

> we take on, through compassion, all the various mental and physical sufferings of all beings: their fear, frustration, pain, anger, guilt, bitterness, doubt, and rage, and we give them, through love, all our happiness, and well-being, peace of mind, healing, and fulfillment.[30]

Was this *Tonglen* so different from Jesus' sharing completely in the joys and sufferings of his friends? Now, it is true that I had received guidance from some Buddhist teachers who saw emotional experience in a more solipsistic way, as entirely one's own private experience and responsibility. Some of them did indeed speak about inner experience as if it were entirely divorced from the external world and from an *ultimate and essential* connection to relationship, society and action. But gradually I became more trusting of those Buddhist mentors who emphasized our deep connectedness to one another and viewed emotion as an important element in it. With their help, I gradually began to understand that emotion per se is not the problem, but rather our relation to emotion. Many of us are driven by our emotions. We are too often unaware of their origins and how to manage them in a way that is consistent with our values. The best Buddhist practices show us how to be intimate with our feelings without losing ourselves in them, all the while remaining completely, positively related to the world and one's social commitments. I was confident that Jesus and Eckhart would affirm these Buddhist values.

When we lose what we love most—our jobs, loved ones, possessions, and even our identities—we are humbled and naked before God. Then, when the floor of our personal grief breaks open into the universal, we instantly see that *everyone* has lost or is losing something or someone who is dear and precious. No one is exempt. In such moments of clear insight, we find the grief-stricken ones, the murderers, the joyous dancers, the liberators, and the hopeless, homeless ones within ourselves. If we undergo our emotions with attention, we can know these universal human territories intimately and with a clarity that comes only from direct experience. The dimension of universality is not merely a nice philosophical notion. Medieval Christian mystics such as William of St. Thierry (twelfth century C.E.) conceived of the human person as a microcosm of the universe. To know oneself experientially in God was to know something universal—human nature itself—made in the image of God.[31] In scripture, that essential connectedness is called the Body of Christ.

For me, Rebecca's baptism just moments before her death exemplified the existential bridge from private to universal suffering. That water, flesh, and blood blessing fell like a stone into a still lake, sending out ripples of grace through Rebecca to everyone, and from everyone to her, from and to the heart of all creation in God. My fingertips became God's. Rebecca's forehead became mine. Her forehead became Sam's, Christy's, Marg's, Mom's, Dad's, my great grandparents' and the forehead of each of my innumerable, invisible ancestors and descendants. My tears were theirs and God's as well in the *Now* of God which Eckhart so prized. Why didn't Eckhart see that emotions, rather than being a threat and an attachment, could be the milieu of the cosmic *Now*? I wondered how to convince him.

Gradually I became aware that I was talking to Eckhart subvocally as I read his work. I argued that when we suffer "in Christ," we open ourselves to Unconditional Love—not as an abstract principle but as a Presence that comes right into our private suffering and feels it with us. I wondered if Eckhart would agree that this ever-present Presence is what the Incarnation is all about! We each have a cross to bear, and sometimes the pain is excruciating. And yet, "My yoke is easy and my burden is light," says Jesus, forever (Matthew 11:30).

In the months after Rebecca's death, I met a few other parents who had experienced their loss in this deeply Christian way. When they surrendered into the grief, they felt as if they were participating in the Body of Christ. One woman told me that, in being accompanied by Christ, she had been born again with him, and that he too was being born again with her. Is this what Eckhart meant when he said that the Son is always being born? Our suffering and transfiguration are Christ's, and Christ's are ours. Those who follow their suffering in this way become Christ-bearers for one another. I was beginning to see that in both Christian and Buddhist practice, true suffering is not a private pain but rather a transpersonal, interdependent experience.

I pushed the point in my inner dialogue with Eckhart. We agreed that one could be sentimental, self-pitying, and attached to various feelings. We also agreed that sometimes one can be more effective in work if emotions are repressed or sublimated. I know artists who, in their personal lives, don't look like emotional people, but their creations are filled with passion and evoke a passionate response in others. And I have several relatives who are surgeons. Quite often their well-deserved reputations as brilliant healers depend on their passionless objectivity. Deep passion can sometimes 'disappear' into a great work of art.

Still, I didn't believe Eckhart took seriously the spiritual, interpersonal, and social damage that results when people are, in an unhealthy way, emotionally detached. Interviews with adolescent killers in Boston reveal kids who have shut off their feelings, their empathic emotional connectors. They can shoot someone in the head, then go out and have a Coke with friends. As I was finishing this book, a bomb blast tore apart the Federal Building in Oklahoma City. One hundred sixty-eight adults and children were killed. The accused murderer, Timothy McVeigh, was shown pictures of the young victims. He had no emotional reaction. One of the policemen who was there reported, "[There was] nothing. Zero reaction from that son of a bitch. This guy is a stone."[32]

The only way I could imagine not mourning so deeply was not to love so much. But could I love less? The poet Robert Burns (1759–1796) expressed the dilemma in a poem called "Ae Fond Kiss":

> Ae fond kiss, and then we sever!
> Ae farewell, and then forever!
> Deep in heart-wrung tears I'll pledge thee
> Warring sighs and groans I'll wage thee....
>
> Had we never lov'd sae kindly,
> Had we never lov'd sae blindly,

Never met—or never parted—
We had ne'er been broken-hearted.[33]

Broken-heartedness seemed to come with the territory of living and loving fully. Of course, my arguments with Eckhart also indicated warring voices within myself. What good was it to love others deeply, knowing that they would eventually die? What good was grief? Better to deny the mysteries of interpersonal longing and love. Perhaps the champions of *apatheia* (Greek, for a contemplative state of mind that completely transcends both everyday emotions and deep passions) such as Evagrius, Eckhart, and Dokyo Etan were right. Better to sit by the river unperturbed and watch the emotions go by, like boats.

In spite of my uncertainty about whose advice to trust, I found myself siding with those Christian mystics who put an ultimate value on the "suffering" of love. They saw it as a high form of suffering, often citing the Song of Songs in Hebrew scripture as the fundamental model for the soul's relationship with God. In the spiritual tradition of the Song, one cherishes the soul's "wound of love," as the joyful/sorrowful result of true intimacy. God is the soul's Beloved, and the soul is God's Beloved. In this tradition, the problem is not undergoing emotional pain as such, but rather clinging to the private, self-pitying suffering that refuses to surrender itself to the Beloved, and thus to the universal Great Suffering, in God. In this tradition, detachment is not an imperious severing of emotional connectedness but rather a gradual surrender of all those worldly, ego loves and small emotions which hinder our complete intimacy with the Beloved.

Discovering the God Within

In moments of despair, I wondered if all my questions about life, death, love, and grief were meaningless. A cold, dark voice counseled, "Sure, you loved Rebecca. Your love *feels* as if it were the final truth, as if nothing could be stronger. But hope is deceptive and illusory. You will die, and that's it, period. People's personal love dies with them. Everything disappears without a trace. Feel your feelings or don't feel them, it doesn't matter. Nothing matters."

Another inner voice took up the challenge. "Wrong. Authentic love really participates in something greater, something that lives eternally. If we keep loving, right through death's doorway, new life springs up. But we must hold nothing back. To love in the presence of death is to cultivate divine *humus*, the ground that brings new life. And the ground is God, ever new. God brings all things into existence and receives them when they pass out of existence. Get out, Death! You have no power here anymore. *You*, death and *You* meaninglessness, are the ultimate illusions!"

Another sympathetic voice, echoing the mystic Thomas Merton, suggested that meaninglessness shouldn't be considered an enemy at all. Merton once wrote, "I cannot discover my 'meaning' if I try to evade the dread which comes from first experiencing my meaninglessness!"[34] My soul had become a spiritual tennis court of Great Voices.

The competitive struggle among these archetypal voices brought me back to the Bible. Jesus was a passionate person. He was touched by the death of Lazarus. He was moved in his love for John and in his love for the criminals on the neighboring crosses. He had said, "I am deeply grieved" (Matthew 26:38). Did Eckhart imagine that Jesus was cool as a cucumber when they drove the nails through his hands? I didn't think so. Wasn't the whole point of the Incarnation that the Great, Unfathomable Mystery *became* our human loneliness, joy, forsakenness, and suffering? God was not an Unmoved Mover, but an intimate participant. God felt it all, exactly as we can feel it. Eckhart said that in Jesus, only the "outer man" suffered. But was Jesus merely pretending to be human—a heresy called "docetism" which the early church condemned? Was my medieval Dominican friend a docetist? I told him, quite frankly, "Maybe your teaching *should* have been condemned!"

Eckhart's preference for dispassionate detachment fit with his view of God in scripture. The mystery of the Godhead was totally transcendent, hidden from our experience, especially our emotional experience, by a cloud of unknowing. No one had ever seen or touched the face of God. I agreed with Eckhart's assessment. As soon as someone says he is certain about what and who God is, that person is almost always an ideologue, attached more to his idea than to God. God is always greater. But Jesus also said, "Whoever has seen me has seen the Father" (John 14:9). Didn't the Incarnation show us what cannot be seen and give us knowledge of what cannot be known? Didn't God experience and communicate the full essence of God's Being and Subjectivity in the human Jesus (and therefore, by participation, in every human being), or did God hold something back?

Some Christians believe that God gave full divinity to Jesus, but not to anyone else. Eckhart and I agreed that this view is not what Jesus intended. People wanted to make him an earthly king, but he told them no. Jesus, speaking out of an "I" that was totally one with God, gave himself unreservedly to others. His oneness with God was not going to be a spiritual possession that separated him from anyone else. In the Gospel of John (chapter 17), Jesus says of those who love him,

> [21]that they may all be one. As you, Father, are in me and I am in you, may they also be in us. . . . [22]The glory that you have given me I have given them, so that they may be one, as we are one, [23]I in them and you in me, that they may become completely one, so that the world may know that you have sent me and have loved them even as you have loved me. . . . [26]I made your name known to them, and I will make it known, so that the love with which you have loved me may be in them, and I in them.

Jesus' "I" was completely interdependent. There was a vast "we" within his "I." I reasoned that if God empties God's Self totally into the historical Jesus, then through him God empties God's Self into every historical person, including me and Rebecca. Jesus wanted us to know that the universal "we" of love and compassion is within everyone's "I." When Jesus says "I am the Way, the Truth and the Life" (John 14:6), it is the "I" of Abba who speaks, the "I" whose love falls on everyone equally, like sun and rain.

"That is the whole point of John's Gospel!" I shouted out loud, as I argued to those imaginary Christian friends who emphasize Jesus' perfection and our sinfulness. I sensed that Eckhart was in agreement. Since, and because of, the Incarnation, every finite thing, person, image, memory, and emotion is made transparent to God, as something actually alive in, and expressive of, God. Individual people and their thoughts, senses, and emotions can be alive with God's holy presence!

I explained to Eckhart that I didn't mean to belittle his view of detachment. After all, I too had glimpsed an equanimity of mind and heart that left the depths of the soul undisturbed. But I knew that many of us suppress and reject some emotions as "unspiritual" even before we thoroughly discern their origin or meaning. For example, as a Lutheran, I grew up in the shadow of the traditional seven deadly sins, according to which all anger was un-Christian. Consequently, I often didn't feel anger even when it was appropriate, and I didn't express it when it was needed. Now it seemed clear to me that the peace that came from judging and suppressing my real emotions was illusory, and I didn't want to repeat that mistake. Now, I was looking for God in my ordinary experience, not "out there" on the clouds.

Luckily, there is another stream of Christian reflection which supported my search. It is exemplified by some of Thomas Aquinas's comments. He wrote in his *Summa Theologica* that anger in itself is not morally wrong. Anger is a complex passion, he said, composed of many emotional currents. One of those currents is a perception of injustice. Anger can be a sign that some injustice is afoot. Anger itself can have the energy and intention of righting a wrong.

Of course anger can be misused, to push others away, to blame them or to do violence to them. As I reflected on my emotional life in the months after Rebecca's death, I regretted moments in my life when I hurt others with my anger, and, where I could, I asked others for their forgiveness. But I tried to remember that anger itself was not the culprit. In Aquinas's view, anger and all the passions are a necessary part of the Christian life when they are directed toward God. In giving them over to God, God comes into our human emotions, enlightening them from within, making them His/Her own. I thought Aquinas's distinctions were good ones. The quality of my anger when I was blaming a poky driver on the highway was decidedly different from the anger that arose when I shook my fist to God about the injustice of Rebecca's brief life. The latter was somehow larger and connecting, rather than isolating. Sometimes, it seemed as if God too was shaking God's fist—as a gesture of love and solidarity—within me.

The Spiritual Practice of Detachment

Eckhart's teachings became like a prism to me, giving off different colors of the spiritual rainbow, depending on where I stood. In the end I read Eckhart's words on detachment as a reminder to sit on my meditation bench, to play the flute, and to pray each day no matter what. Spiritual detachment meant "attachment" to God as Mystery and Love. While instructive and motivating, emotions were also ephemeral, coming and going, moment to moment. I needed a strong, stable, inner reference point for my life. In the regular morning silence dedicated to God, strong emotions often integrated themselves around an invisible center. I didn't have to "get a handle" on them, figure them out, repress them, express them in exorbitant ritualistic ways or arrange them in a cognitive hierarchy of value. I simply put my forehead to the ground and asked for God's love and mercy.

The steady love of God and peace of Christ awaited me, no matter what particular mood or thought happened to be passing through. I recalled the principle I had learned in the Grand Canyon: "It doesn't matter what you think. God's love is always shining in you, in nature and in others, moment to moment. Your thoughts cannot make it happen or save you." Jesus had said, "Do not let your hearts be troubled. I give you a peace the world cannot give" (John 14). The reception of that peace does not depend on our thoughts.

Sometimes, as I sat on my prayer cushion in the early mornings, I received that peace. I began to trust that the deep emotions, whether pleasant or unpleasant, were not mere sentimentality but healing waters of life, coursing through my body, drawing me closer to God. These realizations helped me to reframe Eckhart's idea of detachment. Eckhart thought God's peace was an infinitely reliable, invisible "place" within. He called God's home in the soul, the "Aristocrat." Perhaps he meant that the "Aristocrat" was so interiorly transcendent and so infinitely faithful and trustworthy that it was, as Aristotle had said, the Unmoved Mover in us, like a totally

trustworthy king. God would continue to be the ground of good-
ness, love, mercy, and justice in us, no matter what. And if we had
faith, nothing in this cosmos could separate us from the love of
God. God's face was always turned toward us. Stated in this way, I
saw that there was no incompatibility between the Unmoved God
and Christ, between Aristotle's God and the passionate God of
Hebrew/Christian scripture. *Unmoved* did not mean emotionally
disconnected, but rather the steadiness that one finds in a trustworthy, empathic friend.

Eckhart spoke of an outer and an inner person. He said the inner
person was always undisturbed, in God. But how could there be
such different intensities of feeling between the inner and the outer
person? Where was the boundary, and how could one find the
proper ground of detachment? His notion seemed to require an
impossibly subtle distinction.

I was, therefore, delighted in his elegant, poetic solution. For
him, the inner place of detachment is like

> a door, opening and shutting on a hinge. I compare the planks on the out-
> side of the door with the outer man, but the hinge with the inner man. As the
> door opens and shuts, the outside planks move backwards and forwards,
> but the hinge remains immovable in one place, and the opening and shutting
> does not affect it.[35]

This image seems right to me. Within the soul, there lies an
undisturbed, invisible turning radius. One can be very close to God
in this dynamic stillness, even in the midst of everyday events and
passions. This deep, still hinge of Presence is uncontrollable from
the vantage point of the ego. Its center is in God in us, and yet the
Spirit "blows where it chooses" (John 3:8). To know where it is
blowing, we must listen closely. Then we are able to swing with the
invisible, sacred hinge of Mystery within. Whether that Great Mystery that is God is affected by our personal suffering and joy is a
question that itself resides within the mystery.

When Eckhart Himself Appears

Gradually, Eckhart's presence became more real and intimate.
We preached to one another, shouted at one another, hugged one

another, and wrote each other notes. Was I crazy to believe that my imagination might be a doorway into something transcendent? Was I crazy to believe I might receive spiritual guidance from someone who had been dead for six and a half centuries? Were the moments of spiritual connectedness with others only an imaginary game? Maybe. And yet, somehow, I could not *not* believe that Eckhart's presence was real. I was getting a feel for his personality. I actually felt guilty when I thought I wasn't being fair about his lack of trust in emotions, and I wanted to apologize. When I laughed at his jokes, there was a certain "withness" in the laughing, as if he were there enjoying it too. In my self-doubt, I consulted a trusted Tibetan Buddhist monk. Had he ever had transtemporal experiences like this, about deceased teachers in his lineage? "Oh, yes," he replied. "Great harm comes when we think we are alone."

I told him, "That sounds like something Eckhart would have said," and I felt assured.[36]

One day, as I took my daily walk in the woods, I challenged Eckhart directly on his view of emotions. Seeking to connect with my psychological language, he accused me of "repetition-compulsion." Couldn't I think of something else to talk about? In my prayerful imagination, we laughed heartily as we faced one another and shook each other's shoulders with aggression and delight. The playful intensity of our wrestling reminded me of Sam and me, when we pretended we were bucks, butting our heads together on the living room floor and falling off imaginary cliffs.

Merely reading Eckhart for information was missing the point. On the level of theological information, Eckhart was a confusing jumble of contradictions. He could be read as just another Neoplatonic philosopher who believed in a stoic, otherworldly detachment, a detachment he had once described as a virtue higher than love! (I thought that was a particularly dumb thing for him to say, and I told him so. "Ultimately, there's no difference between them," I said.) But Eckhart's writing was more poetry than prose, more like Beethoven's *Missa Solemnis* than some marching band's rendition of "Onward Christian Soldiers." One read him for the music, not the facts, trusting that there is sometimes more truth in an aria well sung than in a creed precisely parroted.

"Look," Eckhart once said, turning to me with his soft and wild eyes, "the teaching on detachment isn't meant to be a defense against our emotional life but simply a giving in to it, 'without a why.' I agree with you. Deep grief and joy connect us emotionally to other beings and to nature, beneath our thinking and our 'whys.' Too often, we add another layer of unnecessary judgments and comparisons, about ourselves, others, and God. This extra layer of intellectual reaction to our emotions separates us from God. When we detach ourselves from the illusion of intellectual control and empty ourselves into God, we find ourselves riding on a continuously running river of grief and infinite love at the heart of it all.

"I never meant to say we shouldn't grieve." Eckhart went on. "In fact, I meant that when we let go into God, we are, in a sense, *always* grieving. Our personal and momentary griefs and loves are doorways into grieving and loving that have no beginning and no end. I've heard you say it to yourself: Our small grief becomes God's Grief. Likewise, if we experience a truly just motive or a truly just act, we should know that we have come into union with Justice itself, as it is in God. When we practice justice without self-consciousness, we manifest infinite Justice working through us. Even more, then we *are* Justice. The same goes for Mercy, Truth, Love, and Forgiveness. They are God's. They are God."

I laughed my agreement. Eckhart could be outrageous, but I felt he was trustworthy. He had used the twentieth-century Freudian ideas of "repetition compulsion" and "defense" to help me understand his views. I sensed Eckhart's agreement that if we surrendered our concepts about the world, and instead experienced it directly, we found infinite opportunities for love and mourning. In these assumptions he sounded exactly like my Zen teachers, for whom direct experience, moment to moment, was everything. Eckhart had never met a Buddhist, but he did not seem surprised to learn of their teachings. "After all," he offered, in one of our transtemporal conversations, "In all my sermons I spoke as a Christian friar, yes, but I spoke about universal human experience. Anyone who lives into the Great Silence 'without a why' must discover Justice, Beauty, Truth, and Equanimity. Buddhists, like us Christians,

are human beings first. 'God gives to all things alike and as they proceed from God they are alike.'"[37]

And what about mourning, I wanted to know. Eckhart agreed
with my psychotherapeutic assumption that grieving was necessary
for wholeness as a human being. "But for Christians," he continued, "there is the added dimension of the cross. We don't know
what a human being *is* without reference to the birth, life, death,
and resurrection of the Son. We understand what suffering is, by
reference to the Son who is always being born, always being cruci-
fied, in us."

"You remind me of my friend Henri Nouwen," I replied. "Henri
says that what happened to Jesus is happening now, to us. He says
the Holy Spirit is descending to each of us, announcing that we too
are God's beloved sons and daughters. He says that we too are
tempted as Jesus was tempted, called to minister to others just as
Jesus was, called to the cross as he was and finally called into a res-
urrected life, just as he was. Sometimes I think even Rebecca has
gone through that whole spiritual drama. She too was called to
minister, and she did."

I told Eckhart that many Christians today are responding to
Nouwen's work and his, because they both speak optimistically
about human persons and our destiny to experience God directly.
"Perhaps one day I will meet him, and perhaps he would agree that
there is something more," Eckhart interrupted. "It is not only that I
become optimistic. In reality, the optimism is not my own, but
God's. Even I am not my own, but God's, just as you are learning
Rebecca is not your own, but God's. Without God, we are nothing.
When we know this, we are within God's knowing and love and we
become just what God is."

I smiled. "This is where you got into trouble with the Roman
hierarchy, isn't it? Didn't you imply that we are God? Certainly, I am
not God, you are not God, Rebecca isn't God. Right?"

"You are looking in the wrong place for answers, my friend,"
replied Eckhart with an answering smile. We both knew quite well
the opportunities for ego-aggrandizement when one assumes any
kind of equality with God. "I can only repeat to you something said
by Augustine in the fifth century. 'Whatever a person loves, a per-

son is. If he loves a stone, he is a stone; if he loves a human being, he is a human being. If he loves God—I dare speak no further. If I were to say that he was then God, you might stone me. But I refer you to scripture.'"[38]

I laughed, appreciating his humor and his easy manner.

Eckhart continued, "What I mean is that if you join yourself nakedly to God in loving, you become unformed, and then informed and transformed in the divine uniformity in which you are one with God. But you must stay within, where the Son is being born in you. Rebecca has brought you to that place of eternal birth and death. When you are one with God, you bring forth all creatures and by being one with him, you bring happiness to all creatures."[39]

Eckhart told me that true joy and peace come about only if we go straight into the heart of God, naked and totally dependent on the One who declares we are loved, no matter what. We Christians say that the eternal expression of the invisible Godhead is made visible in Jesus. Jesus was a historical person, but when he walked, spoke, ate, slept, and healed, something eternal walked, spoke, ate, slept, and healed. It wasn't merely Jesus' human self or ego doing all these things. This insight prompted me to add, "Many Christians reject your advice because you seem to make us equal to Jesus. They say you . . . ."

"Stop!" Eckhart interjected. "I grow weary of the accusations. Look deeper, for yourself. Jesus told his disciples, 'I call you friends' (John 15:13–15). He told them, 'As the Father has loved me, so I have loved you; abide in my love. . . . I have said these things to you so that my joy may be in you, and that your joy may be complete' (John 15:9, 11). Nowhere does Jesus say, what I have you cannot have, what I am, you cannot be. He doesn't say, 'I've got my joy, you get yours.'"

Had I detected some anger in Eckhart's voice? I couldn't blame him. After all, when he was accused of heresy, he always maintained he loved the church and that his words had been taken out of context. His anger didn't seem vindictive to me. It was not merely an expression of his frustration at not being understood. Maybe he was giving me a lesson in how to be passionate and yet detached. His deep feeling brought me into that field of grace again. I felt the impact of Eckhart's "Stop" as a wake-up call, like Jesus turning over the tables of the temple money changers (John 2:13ff.).

Eckhart saw that many Christians are sleep-walking, rightly seeing God in Jesus but missing God in themselves. Jesus never asked to be idealized or idolized. Jesus himself always pointed to the faith of those who were healed, rather than to his own miraculous powers. Jesus himself always pointed to "Abba" (roughly equivalent to our "Daddy") as being the source of everything he said and did.[40] He was like a pure stained-glass window, transmitting God's Light to us and showing us how to be transmitters of the Light for ourselves and others. Eckhart wanted everyone to know that Jesus never said he was the sole owner of the Light. God's life is given to everyone equally, and we should expect to see it in all things evenly.

"In the end we must give away everything," said Eckhart. "You are learning this great lesson from Rebecca. Someday you must give away all your belongings, your friends and family, and finally your life. That is inevitable. Someday you must even give away scripture and any images you may have of Jesus or God. At a certain point in the spiritual journey, we must 'let go of God, for God's sake.'[41] Eventually, words, images, thoughts, and all sensory experience fall away. Then you will see the Mystery face to face, and the one in you who sees God will be God."

I imagined sitting by a New England riverbank on a warm fall day to talk with my friend Eckhart. He agreed that too much had been made of his emphasis on the cognitive intellect. Cognition was too often aligned with the selfish ego, always comparing and judging itself in relation to others, always concerned with winning and losing. With a smile, he told me, "To let one's thinking emerge as part of our giving birth to Christ in our soul, now that is a sweet joy. Then, thinking becomes thanking." I thought of Heidegger's *Das Denken dankt*. Heidegger discovered that some of the earliest Greek thinkers wrote from a being-state of utter astonishment at existence. Their words arose directly out of the astonishment and expressed it with thanks. Thinking, being, thanking, and words were perfectly integrated. Eckhart knew my heart. Looking out onto the river, our smiles became one with the water, clouds, and sky.

"Both my Buddhist and my Christian teachers said I should let go of thinking," I said, hoping to please him with an agreeable insight. "Maybe," he replied, as he dropped down to the ground, making circles in the dirt with his finger. After some silence, he added, "There's nothing wrong with thinking. Thinking connects us to others, just as emotions do. It is true, much of our thinking is habitual fantasy, but at other times, thought is an icon, a transfiguration, or the foretaste of service. We must stay awake to know the difference." Suddenly I realized that I had myself just recently come to that same insight. It was as if he knew what I was thinking before I really had grasped it.

"O.K.," I finally said after considering Eckhart's words, "so our thinking, our mundane sensations and feelings, moment to moment, are like stained-glass windows within us, transmitting God's light?" Out of the corner of my eye, I saw Eckhart nodding his approval in silence.

"And, when you speak of joy, you mean it, right? That is, it is a joy you can feel, not some mountain of lead detachment. Right?"

As if knowing how deeply I had struggled with his words on detachment, Eckhart reached to touch my arm and whispered, "God is peace itself and beyond peace. I have often said this. But I tell you something else. God takes delight in giving himself away to everyone and to the cosmos, equally. His pleasure is as great, to take a simile, as that of a horse, let loose to run over a green heath, to gallop as a horse will as fast as he can over the greensward—for this is a horse's pleasure and expresses his nature. It is so with God.'[42] The heart of God is dancing ecstasy, and knowing everything simultaneously, in love."

A tear came to my eye. I felt deeply touched and honored to be in the company of this great man. After several moments of prayerful communion, I said, "That's the sort of knowing we're meant to have, right? There is a big difference between having information *about* someone and knowing someone intimately, in love. There is more personal involvement, empathy, and commitment when we know *and* love someone. I can feel in my body how much I love

Rebecca, Sam, Christy, Margaret, and others. It's not a matter of thinking about them in a certain way. In loving them, they are in me, and participating in God's love."

"Yes," replied Eckhart. "That going-beyondness is in you, and in Rebecca too. In that place you are everyone and everyone is you. Sin is the impulse to separate yourself from others, to make them not-you and not-God. Getting information about God or someone is a poor substitute for meeting them face to face. Information objectifies what we are knowing, setting it outside our sphere of intimacy and care. Oh yes, some information, some objective knowledge, is useful, but we need to watch our motives for seeking it. Is our motive sin or service? We sin when we make others different from us and pull them down from their ascent to the universal in God. Sin is making ourselves, others, and God smaller than we really are, according to our own tiny ideas and projections. In our true nature, in God, we do not sin. The love coming from God takes us beyond our ideas *about* God, into the heart of the Mystery we dare not diminish. There is always more."

We fell into the waiting silence. And then I knew that through Rebecca I had glimpsed that Mystery and the love that perfects everything. "But," I added, "there is something unsettled in my feelings about my daughter Christy. I'm afraid that we will never reconcile." After Rebecca's death, Christy didn't want the closeness with me that I wanted to have with her, and it hurt. The future path of our relationship disappeared into an ominous darkness. Examining a blade of grass in his hand, Eckhart replied, "The light is still shining there. Even when there are clouds, the light is always shining. Maybe your stained glass needs a washing." He smiled, looked upward and then at me out of the corner of his eye. "I think a good, cleansing rain will come. Try a little detachment."

Smiling in the warmth of our friendship I replied, "I'm always grieving, you know. I usually don't feel spiritually detached. My only relief is a sudden clarity I sometimes get when I walk down a city street and see how ruthlessly judgmental I often am. Usually I am in a semiconscious state, half alive, putting people into categories. I'm either better or worse than someone else. But since Rebecca appeared, in special moments, I see beneath the surface to the lines of worry and sorrow on people's faces. A few look contented, at peace with life. But in the bodies and faces of many others, I see the constricted breathing and distracted, darting eyes of fear, or the manic, strained backs and overexcited eyes of greed. I see the bent shoulders of someone who is broken by life. Something in me reaches out to them, touching them as I touched Rebecca, in love and compassion. I want to bless them all, and to receive their blessing."

"What are you feeling now?" Eckhart wanted to know.

I thought this was funny, Eckhart asking me about my *feelings*. "I'm not sure how to describe it. Some combination of perfect love and grief, as if all of creation is yearning and groaning. It's good. Usually I'm too distracted by the constant blare of the media and the tree full of monkeys that is my mind." We laughed.

What a pleasure it was, to share such intimacy with my friend Eckhart. I had never known anyone who could listen so clearly and deeply. He nodded and smiled as I told him how Rebecca made it easier to stop and say hello to people I had never met, easier to listen to their stories, easier to understand their pain, easier to offer some compassion. Eckhart and I sat for hours, speaking occasionally, but mostly looking out over the water. Sitting in the light with him was to share in that eternal place where, as he always said, "this and that" disappears: that place where he and I, the river and the boats, the canyon and the mountain, the clouds and the sky, Rebecca and Jesus, are one. In those precious moments by the river, I saw that heaven was a time already here, but not yet.

Henri's Visit

When Henri said he would come to visit in late September if I wanted, I was in one of my "everything-is-fine" moods. I said yes, but privately I thought his visit wouldn't make much difference.

I thought about Henri's idea that this loss was an opportunity to be closer to God. Did I really want to be reminded of that? I realized that my tendency to be emotionally self-subsistent was also true in my relationship with God. Twenty-five years ago, in my first college course on Religion, the professor had described one strain of American deism as a theology of "God-in-the-gaps." God had made the world and then stepped out of it, letting it run like a well-ordered clock. Since the Enlightenment, many of us only turned to God in special emergencies, or to bridge temporary gaps in our understanding or in our hope for progress. I was embarrassed to acknowledge that I had treated both God and my friends that way. They were too often "friends-in-the-gaps." If I weren't totally falling apart, I would not confess my vulnerabilities to them.

When at last Henri did walk in our door, I was able to acknowledge how much I needed him. He reminded me of times I had given him emotional support. Now, he said, it was my turn. A couple of years before he had been struck by a pickup truck. He had almost died, and now he felt as if he had nothing to lose. "A deep sense of trust in God came to me when I lay there at the threshold," said Henri. I hoped some of his faith could rub off on me.

Henri stayed the whole day and into the next afternoon. We established ourselves in different parts of house—the kitchen, my office, the living room, the back porch—talking about life, God, death, friendship, and Jesus. He understood the fear and the desire to escape from the unpleasantness of grieving. And he also affirmed my desperate need to stay close to Rebecca. "Rebecca is showing you something of God's vulnerability. She is as close to God as Jesus is," he said.

I told Henri about a Lakota Sioux friend at the Buddhist-Christian conference who whispered something important to me two days after Rebecca's death. The friend and I were at an ecumenical, East-West service. I told him I was learning from Rebecca. He leaned over and said, "Yes, she can be your teacher." This made sense to Henri, too. Rebecca was a channel of Jesus' grace coming to me. I had held her and now she was with God. I had come that close to God!

As we talked I suddenly remembered the story in Daniel where King Nebuchadnezzar ordered Shadrach, Meshach, and Abednego thrown into the fiery furnace. Later, the king was astonished to see them walking, unhurt, in the midst of the fire. In the face of such a majestic display of God's power, Nebuchadnezzar made a dramatic decree: "Any people, nation, or language that utters blasphemy against the God of Shadrach, Meshach, and Abednego shall be torn limb from limb, and their houses laid in ruins; for there is no other god who is able to deliver in this way" (Daniel 3:19ff.). Those who spoke against God were within me, and I needed a passionate, fiery God who could deliver me from myself. There was a Nebuchadnezzar in me, standing up for the love of God, shaking my fist in the air and denouncing any temptation to meaninglessness and despair. I knew Henri stood up for that God, too. Henri offered an involved, empathic, and intimate God, like a father who would protect his children. Henri's presence reminded me of who I really am: the one whose German Lutheran grandmother taught him to speak by memorizing Christian prayers, the one who always carried in his soul the image of Jesus protecting the lost sheep.

Henri empathized with my realization that life was more terrible than I thought. "That attitude is not entirely a bad thing," he replied. "Life is so painful when we love, but there is a way to stay close to the reality of it. If we stay close to each other and open to God's love, forgiveness, and mercy, then we can bear these things." "You know," I replied, "I've heard you say those things before, but I can hear you much more clearly after this death. Death is like a black worm in the middle of the apple, munching away at the meaning and the desire to live." Henri nodded, and I continued, "But you're right. My salvation is to know that Jesus is there, even in the worm, even in the Nothing."

How true, I thought. The worm was in Jesus and he died. But Jesus was also in the worm. Jesus lived through and beyond the threshold of nothingness.

From Henri I took in a new depth of believing in myself, in love, in friendship, in God and in the process of something important unfolding. I told him about my struggles with Eckhart, especially in the realm of "detachment" and "letting go." He instantly understood that "surrendering" was not so much something I *did* as it was something I *accepted*. Rebecca was torn from us, and it was our work to live fully into that brokenness.

"If you can accept this death, right there in you, brokenness is a gift," Henri offered. Henri understood that the reality of death is too much to bear, but only from its midst, its "too-muchness," do Jesus' life and death make sense.

At dinner, Henri, Marg, and I had the giggles. As Sam played with his toy horses in the living room, the three of us adults sat around the kitchen table telling funny stories. The following morning Henri joined in our family's Sunday morning activities. In his final few hours with us, he sat with Marg out on the back porch while I took Sam. Then, while Sam napped, the three of us reflected on Rebecca's death together. His message was clear and consistent. Rebecca's death was taking us both to a new important level of spiritual closeness with God. God was revealing God's Self to us in her death.

Finally, Henri led us in the Eucharist in the living room. After he had gone, Marg and I felt rejuvenated by his loving presence and friendship. For me, his visit was pivotal. Henri's faith had given me the courage to step over the line, more fully into my Christian life.

Grief and Prayer

In the weeks after Henri's visit I reflected on this Christian God to whom we had committed ourselves. While I felt totally dependent on God, I also felt God was depending on me to live through everything in love. In a sense, God *wanted* to become embodied in Rebecca, me, Henri, Marg, Sam, and everyone, and was receiving something precious from us. God's joy was in seeing each of us become completely transformed. Wasn't that the real meaning of the Incarnation, that we each become Christ from within our particular personalities and circumstances, and then Christs for each other? St. Paul had said, "It is no longer I who live, but Christ who lives in me" (Galatians 2:20), and that we could have Christ Jesus' mind and heart (Philippians 2:5ff.). Weren't we the Body of Christ? Didn't Jesus say that we were to treat others as if they were Christ (Matthew 25:40ff.)? Jesus didn't *own* being Christ and hold it back for himself. Rather, he emptied his Christ nature out so that all creation was set free (Philippians 2:5; Galatians 5:1). Christ himself is set free, through the Holy Spirit, blowing where He/She wills, now appearing in children like Rebecca, now in a friend's presence or in nature.

A friend of mine said God moaned with me. It was somewhat comforting to know that I was accompanied. But accompaniment couldn't erase the pain. Even when Marg and I wept together, no comfort descended into that lonesome, desert-place of suffering in my soul. Seeing Marg's grief did not lessen my own. I tried to trust that only by admitting the full loneliness of the suffering was Christ being born in me, as Eckhart had said. This new birth could only happen if I let go of everything, becoming empty of all my usual supports and comforts, and of Christ. After all, on the cross, even Christ emptied himself of Christ (Philippians 2:5–11). The notion that Christ could only be born in me if I carried the cross of Jesus' apparent abandonment of our family didn't make sense intellectually. It was a growing heart-perception.

This deeper, more subtle sense of Christ's presence spoke to me in a story told by one of the participants in a men's group that I led some time after the death. Tom, a pastoral counselor, told me about a friend of his, a fundamentalist minister whose beloved wife was dying of cancer. One day the minister came to visit his wife in a small, inner-city hospital. When he walked into the room, he saw her staring, glassy-eyed, at a red, blinking neon sign across the street. "Jesus Saves!" winked on and off, splashing red light across her eyes. The husband stopped, looked, and walked deliberately over to the window, yanking down the shade. "That's not gonna work anymore!" he announced angrily. He knew that the sentimentalized, idolized Jesus he used to believe in was not going to save his wife, at least not in any literal sense. This story made a deep impression on me. Here was someone who could let go of the Jesus he had known and turn instead to the stark reality of his wife and their common brokenness. In his sudden loneliness and "lack of faith," he was closer to God than ever. He could let go of the saving Jesus who is preoccupied with our sins and turn instead toward the Jesus who lovingly loses himself in our suffering and is willing to die with us, emptying himself of unreachable grandeur.

According to Eckhart, emptying ourselves of everything that separates us from God is a kind of holy pregnancy. Pregnant with what? I was learning from the Christian contemplative tradition that when we surrender our illusory hopes in anything less than God, then a vast space opens within us where *God's* hope can be born. I felt comforted by the words of St. John of the Cross in "The Ascent of Mt. Carmel":

> To reach satisfaction in all
> desire its possession in nothing
> To come to the knowledge of all
> desire the knowledge of nothing
> To come to possess all
> desire the possession of nothing
> To arrive at being all
> desire to be nothing.
> To come to the pleasure you have not
> you must go by a way in which you enjoy not
> To come to the knowledge you have not
> you must go by a way in which you know not.[43]

Almost three centuries later, T. S. Eliot echoed St. John's words in "East Coker":

> I said to my soul, be still, and wait without hope
> For hope would be hope for the wrong thing; wait without
>   love
> For love would be love of the wrong thing; there is yet faith
> But the faith and the love and the hope are all in the waiting.
> Wait without thought, for you are not ready for thought:
> so the darkness shall be the light, and the stillness the
>   dancing.[44]

Surrendering to the stillness may seem terrifying and lonely at first, but soon a deeper connectedness with God and others arises. It simply arises—we don't have to make it happen. I figured this movement from separateness and apparent hopelessness to union and joy made theological sense. God creates us to be independent of God because God's joy comes when we, with our separate freedom, seek God alone.

Sometimes I got stuck in my personal grief, in my personal hope that Rebecca should have lived: stuck in the perception of a personal injustice. I was feeling sorry for myself, holding on to my private pain. I simply forgot about God. But soon I would wake up to the Presence and see that I was participating in the prodigal son story over and over—running away, collapsing in failure and self-disgust, and then returning laden with guilt and, surprisingly, being welcomed. Then, a new level of closeness with God came over me. I realized that the very source of my complete *autonomy* as a mature person was in my *union* with God. There was nowhere to go that God *wasn't*. When I lost myself in God I found my true self.

Eckhart wrote that we are created in the trinitarian image of God and that there is a laughing within the Trinity.[45] This divine mirth is an expression of joy that our true selves are participating in God's eternal Being. Perhaps, if we were to perceive correctly, joy is always welling up in our depths, even in the midst of our suffering. Both Buddhism and Christianity call attention to the ubiquitous nature of suffering: it is everywhere and constant. And both declare that there is a release from within suffering. Suffering is not a bad thing in Christian spirituality. When the suffering is in God, it is one birthplace of holy joy, bringing us closer to ourselves, others, and God. Spiritual maturity isn't a complete separation *from* unpleasant emotions, but rather a new level of freedom experienced *from within* them. Maybe, because God is in the depths of our soul, we can experience God's grief and enjoy God's enjoyment directly.

I knew that I needed to have more conversations with Eckhart about these things. I loved him, but I continued to be irritated by how quickly he wanted to disappear into God. Mostly he espoused unity and decried the spiritual immaturity of dwelling in differences, distinctions, and sufferings. Why did he want to rush so quickly past our concrete, human experiences of emotion, perception, and imagination? Why didn't he write about his everyday relationships and the real conflicts of intimacy he experienced? After all, you can't have union if you don't have separate experiences to *join*. Doesn't joy arise because distinctions are celebrated and transcended rather than obliterated? Christian grief is a joining of distinct emotions such as sorrow and joy, hope and hopelessness, love and hate: in these joinings, the personal meets the universal. Christian community too is a joining of preciously distinct human persons. And finally, death is a participation in the union of history and immortality. God is present in all such joinings, by grace; and we humans are present in all such joinings, through prayer. These joinings *are* prayer.

One late September afternoon I suddenly had no energy. I was supposed to lead a therapy group in the evening, but I felt weak and didn't think I could do it. The simplest housekeeping task was a monumental challenge. Walking through the door into my office, tears began streaming from my eyes. I staggered over to the prayer cushion and plunked myself down.

It was often like this. I could never know ahead of time when I needed to cry or to pray with Rebecca. The feelings would suddenly strike in different parts of my body. Some days, the body was numb; on other days, body sensations flowed in eddies of intensity, pleasant and unpleasant, one after another. On still others, I lay almost paralyzed in gut-wrenching pain. In my mind's eye, I often saw Rebecca on the hospital table trying to breathe. Now, I was surprised and a bit embarrassed to notice an impulse to touch my forehead. I hesitated, feeling I might violate a taboo. Maybe I associated a gentle self-touch with masturbation or narcissism. Somehow, I let myself caress the furrow between my eyes as if I were both the giver and the receiver. A blessing was being passed. Suddenly I remembered making this same intimate contact with Rebecca as she lay dying. The sign of the cross formed itself between my brows, just as it had been formed upon Rebecca. If she had lived, she might have liked this comforting touch from her father.

I made the sign on my own forehead now, slowly, over and over. Recalling the Gospel of John, I felt certain he, the beloved disciple, understood such holy moments of body prayer. Who was being caressed? Surely it was me, but it was also Rebecca who lived in me, the other babies on the intensive care floor on the night of her death, and all new beings around the world. Again, it was St. John who came to mind. From this inward, interconnected place of prayer, he wrote, "I am in my Father, and you in me, and I in you" (John 14:20). With the Spirit came a complete, joyful union of new, reborn identities in love. It became clear to me that grieving in God breaks down our old, defensive identities, thus allowing greater, interdependent identities to be born. In authentic prayer our history and old identities are becoming conscious and then returning to the divine soil in our souls. In that "soul-soil," new identities are sprouting.

I had been baptized by a Methodist minister in the summer of 1947. Now, I retraced the mark of that baptism, the mark that united me to Jesus' parental Mystery and to all God's children. Still touching my forehead, I sensed my father's face in mine, and mine in my daughter's. A blessing was being passed up and down the generations. I sensed that all my ancestors were sitting in that room with me, all of us touching Rebecca's forehead, blessing her, and all of us being blessed in return. My forehead was Rebecca's, and simultaneously I was receiving the tender touch of my loving father as I died. Here I was, dying in my father's arms, knowing and wanting nothing else. I was astonished again to realize that loving and mourning were two sides of the same coin. For the first time, I understood that for a Christian, there is no other way but through the cross. Through the loss and the grief, through the abandonment and surrender, come beauty and a transformed life. One's every action, thought, and emotion become prayer, a divine/human communication. I hated it, but I resolved to cling to Christ as we negotiated the narrow passage together.

A Man's Experience of Anger and Grief

Trying to Find the Feeling

In America, it has become a cliché to notice that women, more than men, find it easier to feel and to speak about vulnerable emotions like shame, sorrow, and hurt. At Wellesley College, near Boston, the Stone Center has gathered a group of psychologists such as Jean Baker Miller, Janet Surrey, and Judith Jordan, whose working hypothesis seems to be that women, more than men, experience emotion and self-understanding in the context of intimacy and relationship.[46] We men tend to see ourselves as separate from others, often communicating more abstractly, in contexts of competition. In the 1980s, men such as Robert Bly, Sam Keen, and James Nelson wrote popular books about how men need to expand the range of their emotional repertoire.[47] Today, everyone gets the ironic joke and laughs when, in a popular T.V. sit-com, a twenty-something couple negotiates the next step in their dating relationship with the following repartee:

He (looking down shyly): "You know, I'm not afraid to cry."

She (sitting up straight, looking straight at him): "That's good because I'm not afraid to hurt you."

It is a good thing the public conversation about gender differences has become more commonplace. Joking about the perceived differences is sometimes a good way to diffuse the tension, anger, and hopelessness that can arise between men and women. On the other hand, many people think that our humor about the situation hides a sense of being stuck. Where should the public conversation go from here? As I emerged from the darkest days of grief, this question arose as an important lens for understanding my emotions. Was there something particularly masculine about my struggle with the grieving process? I wasn't sure, but I thought I might discover something helpful for me and for others if I recorded specific qualities of my emotions each day in a journal. In addition to the cultural and psychological questions about emotions, I was also aware of Christianity's history of ambivalence concerning emotional life.

Many of my clients struggled with expressing and interpreting their emotions and understanding the role of emotions in spiritual growth. For example, while anger seems to be an essential element of genuine Christian grief, it is not always easy to recognize one's anger or to channel it in nondestructive ways. How can anger support the grief process rather than repress it? Our inward experience of anger and its subsequent expression can be either a rejection of God or an encounter with God. Likewise, our anger can push others away and hurt them, or it can bring us and others back into community. What was my grieving teaching me about anger?

One Saturday morning I stood washing dishes at the kitchen sink when I noticed an uncomfortable feeling. I tried to put the subtle feeling into words: "I don't want to do these dishes," I said to myself. "I hate them. The sooner I'm through with them, the better." Immediately I realized this was exactly the same destructive anger I sometimes felt when, on the way to a pressing appointment, I encountered a red traffic light. In such moments, nothing mattered but my wanting to get somewhere else. People were simply obstacles to my desire. My personal goals became the standard by which I measured others' value to me. I realized that this angry, compulsive desire to get somewhere, depersonalized everything and everybody. In such moments I was completely cut off from any awareness of God.

Now, at the sink, I caught myself in the act. Or rather, the larger Self's awareness caught my obsessed ego in the act. Because I only wanted to get through these dishes, their separate existence was reduced to being obstacles to *my* freedom. They had become symbols of an emotional imprisonment I resented. Yet in the same moment that I noticed this objectifying, destructive anger, it dissipated. Perhaps grace descended on me at the kitchen sink. I realized I didn't need to go anywhere else at that moment. I could simply wash the dishes. If I was in a prison cell—that is, my skin—could I stop fighting it and surrender to reality?

I paused and took a breath. Now I could see the feeling rather than being possessed by it.

I thought, "This is not about dishes. I would be feeling this badly no matter where I was or what I was doing. What is this anger about?"

I stepped into the pantry to put some plastic bags into a paper bag. My hands were in yellow rubber gloves, wet from the dish water. Every time I tried to put some bags into the paper bag, the gloves stuck to the plastic. I had no patience for this! Punching the pile of plastic bags down with my angry fists, I shouted "Grrrrr! Damn you! Damn you! Damn you!" with increasing intensity. I felt the satisfaction of letting go into the emotion, just as it was. But I also felt guilty about this unreasonable display. I wanted to know the meaning of the anger.

Stepping back from the bags, I asked myself, "Is this still about Rebecca's death? Or is it about that unpleasant, unfinished conversation with my client Carl yesterday?" I knew that sometimes I became angry when I felt helpless. "Do I feel helpless right now?"

Putting the last clean, wet dish into the sink, I decided to get out of the house. Perhaps I could do it in a way that wasn't an escape. I got into the car to run an errand. Then, on the way home, I remembered I often had experienced sorrow *within* or *beneath* my rage. Was I avoiding sorrow? Deciding to check it out, I popped Fauré's *Requiem* into the car stereo. At the first sound of violins, tears dripped down my cheeks. My body relaxed. "Bullseye," I said out loud. It wasn't merely the release of tension that comforted me. My tears expressed a perfect mixture of sorrow and joy that transcended me. It was as if Christ were weeping through me. These tears were the real me, and the real me was united with Fauré's real self and God.

I wondered, "Why is it so hard to know what I am feeling and to stay in touch with who I really am?" "Why does an apparently hard-hearted anger obscure my vulnerability?"

When I got home I locked the door and got out the picture album of Rebecca's birth and death. I would go directly to the pain. Putting the *Requiem* on our home audio system, I sat down to look at the pictures. Tears flowed. I held the *shakuhachi* out in front of me, then put it down, remembering how I had played for Rebecca when she was alive inside Marg, and again in the funeral home and at the burial; remembering how I knelt over her grave in the rain, holding up the flute and vowing to avenge her death through love.

Was I angry at God? I tried shouting, "Damn You, Damn You," as I sobbed and moaned. Now I was getting closer to home. The anger that had crackled off my fingertips all morning long was a surface storm rolling over an inner landscape of profound grief.

Then I remembered something one of my psychoanalytic professors had told me at Harvard ten years before. She had said she didn't have a clue as to where my anger was. Looking back, I could see that my anger had been deep inside me all my life, hiding in the shadows of my psyche. After some years of psychotherapy, I began to remember more clearly how, as a seven-, eight-, and nine-year-old child, I used to awake in the middle of the night hearing shouting, curses, accusations, and the thumps of bodies being pushed against the walls. That little boy, growing up in an alcoholic household, was still alive within me, covering his head with blankets and pillows, desperately hoping his mom and dad wouldn't kill each other.

All of my adult life I had been afraid of anger and angry people. Assuming that anger always led to violence and a break in relationships, I rarely expressed it. Perhaps the eight-year-old in me decided he would never be angry *like that.* Unfortunately, that unconscious decision sent all my angry feelings into exile, whether they were appropriate or not. If I were angry, I couldn't feel it. If I felt it, I couldn't express it. Swallowing anger became a virtue. But there was a cost. Occasionally it would burst out at those I loved in hurtful ways, or at some public figure, or at myself, and anger's aftermath always left me burdened with remorse and guilt.

Now I could see that anger is dangerous only when it is experienced in its superficial manifestation. If one follows anger, even rage, to its roots, one always arrives at a vulnerable place. At the root of rage one often finds hurt. Anger might be a signal that we, or someone we know, is being hurt. If the wrong is then addressed appropriately, some truth is revealed and the feeling of anger drops away. Perhaps we are a victim of injustice or witness to an injustice.

Anger can be an appropriate, holy protest! Anger can be a barometer of interpersonal, political, and spiritual events. I knew that some spiritual guides perceived anger as an entirely negative emotion. They taught that by expressing it, one merely cultivated it. But I felt that the anger arising in the wake of Rebecca's death was often a sacred variety of that emotion, coming out of the heart of love.

It became clear to me that anger had two faces. There was indeed a godly dimension in anger, which came to light if I let go into the depths of human vulnerability and need beneath it. But sometimes I struggled in the clutches of a violent and destructive anger, where everything became an "it" in relation to my immediate needs. Perhaps this variety is properly called rage. I saw that under certain conditions of stress, I might kill for greed or because I hated someone in the moment. It scared me to realize that often it was easier for me to feel rage than to acknowledge more vulnerable feelings, like hurt, shame, or a desire to be held.

I doubted I would ever act on the murderous rages, but didn't we all have a breaking point? I prayed for the grace to use the power of anger wisely. As a psychotherapist and leader of men's groups, I had worked with many men who noticed a similar pattern of anger masking hurt and grief. War is the historically accepted method we men use to deny our grief. We would rather blame and kill others than face our vulnerability and need for others. War is a willful strategy to end these uncomfortable feelings forever by removing the objects of our rage. But, of course, it never works in the long run. War brings even more suffering. I saw clearly that my occasional outbursts of rage at the dishes, stop lights, and slow drivers concealed grief. On this particular October afternoon, after praying over Rebecca's pictures, saying good-bye and crying, I didn't feel angry anymore. A deep somatic peace arose in me.

Playing the *shakuhachi* could surface, clarify my emotions, and bring peace too. As I stepped away from the sink into the pantry, I thought, "I must go to the flute immediately." Playing the flute was not a hobby anymore, but a spiritual calling and sacred discipline. If I violated my vows to Rebecca, my family, friends, community, or flute, I suffered a distance from my own true self, and between myself and God.

Spiritually, being true to my commitments required that I work through anger and grief to their divine source within me. I saw two dangers ahead if I didn't: First, if I allowed only the rage out, I could hurt myself or others. I could get stuck in blaming others—the DES, the doctors, Marg, myself, or God. And second, acknowledging and feeling *all* the emotions that come along in grief was an alternative to depression. Indeed, I flirted with depression: I would simply hide inside myself, insulated from the hurt. I would not extend myself in love to anyone, because that would only lead to more hurt. Fortunately this temptation never got the upper hand. I give credit to my wife Marg and to all the friends and mentors who urged me to go forward into the pain. The problem I faced was that I often did not know when the pain would come, or how it would appear.

Surrendering to the Grief

I learned that if I wasn't true to the grieving process, the rest of my life wouldn't work. In October, I gave a sermon at Marg's church that didn't go well because I believed that I had grieved enough. Trying to put Rebecca behind me, I didn't mention her in the sermon. But then, vaguely aware that I wasn't being straight with myself or with the congregation, I imagined that the parishioners were watching me critically as I spoke. Fumbling in self-consciousness, I almost knocked over the podium. Feeling like a third-grader in his first school play, I spoke haltingly, as if embarrassed. After the sermon I realized my mistake. I had been merely pretending to be normal and to say the right, holy things.

Looking for a way to dive beneath the denial, I developed a mantra, repeating, "Surrender to the grief," with every out-breath. Gradually, the breath reminded me that things were not "normal," and never would be. Rebecca had really died, and even my own breathing was temporary. The lack of feeling didn't mean that I wasn't grieving. Trying to counteract the urgent wish to be productive in my work again, I continued to experiment with ways to discover my real feelings.

One day, as I drove into Boston on the way to a presentation, I realized I felt numb. To the men of my childhood days, numbness could be an asset. It allowed them to get up, morning after morning, even when years of unmet needs and unconscious resentments, losses, rages, dreams, and fears stirred within them. Rivers of feeling moved quickly, silently out of their bodies into the hammers, paint brushes, knives, and wrenches of their trades. My great-grandparents were Wisconsin dairy farmers. One grandfather was a housepainter all his life, and the other was a butcher. I remember tender-hearted moments with them, and I sensed the pride they took in their work and their contribution to the family and community. But often, when they let their emotions become visible, I saw most vividly the anger. Now I saw them within me, saw that I had inherited the masculine fear of vulnerability from my male forebears. Could I change these patterns in myself? Should I?

Noticing the lack of feeling in this particular freeway-moment, I instantly remembered my new identity as a grieving father. Could some intense emotions be just under the surface? Once again I turned to music. Seeking to invite the grief out of the shadows, I put on the audio-tape of Eric Clapton's *Tears in Heaven*. Clapton had written this song for his four-year-old son who died a tragic death. The beautiful, musical lament stirred my heart and soon tears were flooding my eyes. I tried to stay focused on the road ahead, but, lost in my feelings, I missed a crucial exit ramp. "No wonder Grandpa Radenz, the housepainter, put his vulnerable feelings aside during the day, I thought. "What bizarre colors might have appeared suddenly on his customers' walls? No wonder Grandpa Jonas, the butcher, wasn't in touch with his feelings. How much work could he have done if he had wept over every carcass?" I remembered sneaking inside the shadowy, damp slaughter house next to his butcher shop. Once I saw a man shoot a horse in the head. I'll never forget how the man looked away from the horse's eyes when he pulled the trigger. Here was an important metaphor for those of us who spend our brief lives *doing*, with never a thought for *being*.

When we slow down to *be*, to look ourselves in the eyes, it is more difficult to continue our self-destructive ways.

By now I had mistakenly entered the on-ramp for the Massachusetts Turnpike, and was heading west toward New York, 180 degrees away from my audience. Exiting the freeway and turning around, I realized I would need to make better judgments about where and when to feel the pain.

Missing the freeway exit taught me something about the limits of grieving, for myself and for men in general. It was a lesson I had learned years earlier as a beginning therapist: to be an effective listener, I needed to free up my attention for the other person, trusting that my personal feelings would be addressed elsewhere. This was certainly true in other, everyday circumstances. Sometimes we needed to put the full expression of our emotions on hold. My concern was for those men who had put their feelings on hold for so long that feelings had virtually disappeared from the screen of their awareness. These reflections brought me back to Eckhart and his notion of spiritual detachment.

Seeking a Divine/Masculine Archetype of Emotion

"My dear friend, Eckhart," I prodded, "what if your theology of detachment is really an unconscious biology of testosterone? Isn't it apparent that we men are more likely to emphasize detachment than are women? Today, I am trying to discern what part of your teachings are the Word from Eternity and what part are mere sociological expressions of your culture. Notice how many women in your own Rhineland mystic circles spoke about God in terms of bridal imagery, about our relationship to God as a passionate love affair! Is it mere coincidence that almost all Christian mystics who speak of detachment have been men?"

Figuring that Eckhart needed a little post-feminist update, I continued, "In our Western culture we men begin to find ourselves when we leave behind the strong love-attachment to our mothers. Our burgeoning, public identities are born in detachment. No young man wants to be called a 'momma's boy.' We find our identities in separation, in going out to the known world's boundaries. Our destiny is to create and to defend families, enterprises, and territories. Traditionally, the work of the mother is to be a nest for the children. Her identity is relational in the matrix of the nest, while the father, at a distance from the emotional needs of the children, works with other men along a competitive frontier of controlled anger. We men are generally happy to escape the home, where the women and children lose themselves in each other."

"Oh, Eckhart," I cried out, "if you had had a wife and children, you would not have given a detached, empty Godhead such prominence." I sensed Eckhart's vague presence and that he was warming to this psychotherapist's perspective on spirituality. "When you make emptiness the source of everything, people imagine it to be a model for living. People think, 'If the Godhead is an Unmoved Mover or a mountain of lead, then I should be too.' But of course, that's a terrible mistake! I like your 'dancing, laughing Trinity' image best of all. It is an image we mortals can bring to life in our sexual and sensual intimacies, and in our families."

Now I was sure that I had Eckhart on the run. "I wonder, did you emphasize passionlessness because you were celibate? Had you been happily married, would metaphors of surrender into passion and creativity have poured forth from your pen? Would you have found God's presence in the sexual pleasures of the marriage bed, in the wild, bloody nest of a mother whose umbilical cord is still attached to her newborn, in the chaos of a passionate, loving household, or in the naked Indian warrior's proud circling around a campfire? You and your empty Godhead! Perhaps the Godhead's supposed emptiness and stillness are merely a projection of solitary monks who have become resigned to their lonely fate."

"Hold it. Hold it," interrupted Eckhart. "Talk about projections! I appreciate when you don't stereotype me. Sometimes you talk on and on to your idea of me, without giving *me* a chance to respond. You act as if I were a mere projection of yours, as if I were dead!"

"Touché!" I exclaimed as we laughed.

Eckhart continued, "Your reasoning troubles me for two reasons. First, I'm not so sure that men are more emotionally distant than women. Recall St. Teresa of Avila (which for me is an anticipation—she hasn't been born yet!), who said that she wasn't in the least bit emotional and that she sometimes chastised herself for her hardness of heart."[48] Second, I never meant to say that everyone should sit quietly in a monastery. 'If you think that you are acquiring more of God in inwardness, in devotion, in sweetness and in various meditation methods than you do by the fireside, in the stable, or in church, then you are acting as if you took God and ruffled his head up in a cloak and pushed him under a bed. It is not what we do that makes us holy, but we ought to make holy what we do.'[49] God's stillness isn't somewhere else. It is always in the midst of everything—even aggression."

"Think about it. You say that the idea of spiritual detachment is a masculine projection. If everything I think, create, and imagine is merely *conditioned* by biology—masculine or feminine—then what's the point of living? Any human meaning would be mere artifice and sentimental rationalization. Then freedom would be mere fantasy. Surely, consciousness includes, but is also more than, biology. Detachment is not merely a patriarchal act of separating or distancing. Rather, it is a universal state of consciousness in which our knowing—and feeling!—is not dictated by our conditioning. We see and feel things freshly in each moment, as they are, not simply for their use-value to us."

"You're right," I replied. "How amazing that free consciousness can arise out of biology. Without freedom, all our theology, art, music, visions of human wholeness, and visions of God would be merely conditioned expressions of biological energies. Our freedom requires a ground of the ultimate Unconditioned, the Ultimately Free."

Eckhart nodded and continued, "Much of our lives is conditioned, it is true. Many of us walk around as if sleepwalking. We think we are making choices, but in actuality we have resigned ourselves to a shallow fate. We mistake choices about consumer items for real choices. Real choices involve who we are, how we are to live, and whether or not we respond to God's call to Freedom and Love. If we allow ourselves to be reduced to the label "consumer," we are merely waiting for our dismal fate to run its course. Sad, but true. We Christians hold up the image of the resurrection. Many detractors see the resurrection as a sentimental hope, don't they? But it expresses something vital to human survival. It shows us that death, the ultimate direction of all biology and conditioning, is not the last word, and we needn't fear it. I love Jesus' parable about the spring of eternal waters that is in us. That is the wellspring of eternity, the source of new life in each moment. Detachment is living in the freedom of the Unconditioned and Uncreated. When we are truly detached, all of our experience is God's. Our joy is God's, as are our suffering, grief, and anger."

"O.K. I hear you. But here again, aren't these ideas heretical, according to the church? You say that there is something Uncreated within us, as if we were, essentially, God." I remembered that Eckhart had been accused of heresy in the Bull of Pope John XXII, *In Agro Dominico*, dated 27 March 1329. I knew he had suffered greatly under the threats of this Inquisition.

After a moment of silence, Eckhart added, "Yes, my accusers had said I 'wished to know more than is necessary.'"

"And what was that?" I asked.

He smiled. "Truth. I was hungry for truth! There were several accusations. The most painful criticism was their rejection of my sense that there is a something in the mind that is uncreated, unconditioned, and uncreatable. There is something in us. . . ."

Eckhart turned to me, looked down and tugged at my sleeve. "There is something in us, in our cells, male and female, that is not a something at all, but the 'empty' Source of all somethings. I say it is a something, but it is not a thing at all. There is something in us that participates in God, shares in God, and is totally free in God. Because the Source of everything, even of God, is the Godhead, of which we can say nothing. In fact, the Godhead is Nothing, that is, No-Thing. Would it be easier for you if I emphasized freedom rather than detachment?"

"Yes, much easier," I responded immediately. "After all, isn't that the essence of detachment, always to be becoming free? When we are free, then only God knows what and who we are becoming, because we have surrendered our control and our ideas about who we are, to God." I watched Eckhart closely to see if he would agree.

"And isn't that what the Christian scriptures are ultimately pointing toward? Don't St. John and St. Paul say, over and over, 'Christ has set us free?'[50] Unfortunately, institutions, religious or otherwise, aren't crazy about liberated people. Institutions inevitably focus on power and control, propagating their own story line. They are looking for agreement, not freedom. It's a very human thing that we do, but when we humans take control of truth, then God's real Mystery and Freedom are obscured. A liberated person can find Christ in a Protestant church as much as in a Roman Catholic or an Orthodox one. And even more, can't we find Christ in a Hindu temple, Jewish synagogue, Middle Eastern mosque, or Japanese Zendo? Or in nature, the bedroom, or the school? Jesus said, "The wind blows where it chooses. . . . So it is with everyone who is born of the Spirit" (John 3:8). The egos who run many churches want to control where God is!"

It seemed that I had Eckhart's deep attention. Something in the gentle way he listened reminded me of a story in the Gospel of John (chapter 8). A group of religious leaders accuses a woman of adultery and is about to stone her to death. These leaders know of Jesus' respect for Jewish law, but also of his great compassion. Hoping to trick him into abandoning his spiritual commitments, they turn to him and demand, "What do you say?" Jesus bends down and writes with his finger on the ground. When they keep on questioning him, he straightens up and says to them, "Let anyone among you who is without sin be the first to throw a stone at her." Out of Jesus' deep listening, he catches the religious leaders off guard, catches them in their hardness of heart, and they walk away. Eckhart listened like that, and I felt ashamed that I had cast stones at the Christian churches when it is they who baptized me, introduced me to Jesus, and carried on the great, liberating Christian tradition.

Eckhart indicated that he was interested in my attention to men's spirituality. It was a new question for him and he wanted to return to it for a moment.

Picking up on his interest, I continued, "The problem I see is that your teaching of spiritual detachment is getting misused by men in particular as an excuse for emotional denial. Perhaps, for biological and cultural reasons, our penchant for emotional denial expresses an archetypal truth. There is a restlessness in us men that almost requires us to leave behind our tender feelings, propelling us outward, to compete and to conquer. Maybe it's merely hormonal. On the other hand, the role of male-conqueror/protector seems archaic in a capitalist, urban, and information-age culture. Have we men created a modern culture in which we ourselves are an anachronism? Maybe my hope is naïve. But I think that we men can be emotionally vibrant and connected with others while being simultaneously autonomous and spiritually detached. There doesn't *have* to be a contradiction here. I wonder if it is time we sculpted the male archetype in a different direction. Can we men direct our warrior tendencies toward protecting others and the earth, while simultaneously staying in touch with our emotions and needs for intimacy?"

I continued, not wanting Eckhart to think that I undervalued the masculine identity. "I think that our masculinity is a wonderful gift. I enjoy working on machines, doing projects with other men, talking about the latest technologies. We men are good at working side by side with other men, focusing on the work rather than relationships or our feelings about each other. I like that about us. But too often we men become helpless and we regress when we do step into the realm of emotion and intimacy. I think we can bring these worlds together within ourselves. In America, men in positions of power often are scornful of anything tender or vulnerable. They call it "touchy-feely." Actually, I feel that way about sentimentalism, when emotions are small and self-centered. But now, when we men have created and disseminated ultimate weapons of mass destruction, can the planet afford a blanket cynicism about our vulnerability and need for the care of others?"

Eckhart replied, "I see what you are getting at. True spiritual detachment cannot mean coldness of heart or a flight from intimacy. That's not what I meant. Passion is good and compassion is good. But they must be grounded in God's Freedom. When we are free, we can see ourselves and others as we really are and not be attached to any particular result for ourselves. Spiritually, this is true for both men and women. Seeking the Ground of the Unconditioned is a discipline for both. Now, I know that many people in your age criticize St. Paul for his masculine bias, but remember, he also said that, fundamentally, when we are in Christ, 'There is no longer Jew or Greek, there is no longer slave or free, there is no longer male and female; for all of you are one in Christ Jesus' (Galatians 3:28). Spiritual detachment is having that kind of 'indifference': To love without distinction."

"Right. It is a discipline for anyone to become empty of God for God. It means taking a risk to live at the frontier of the unknown, reaching out into the unknown, listening into the unknown, with each other." I figured Eckhart knew everything I was talking about, and more. Now, I wanted him to confirm my understanding. "Isn't this what St. Paul meant when he wrote that Christ *emptied* himself?[51] I'm sorry that so many Christians think your emptiness is nihilistic, but isn't it entirely Christian, even more Christian than those who thump their Bibles on the streetcorner, and shout Jesus' name? We never know how the Holy Spirit will show up, do we? Being empty is a not-knowing, a letting go of our conditioned responses so something truly spontaneous can arise. You want us to let go of our concepts *about* God and to find God as God actually is. In the same way, to let go of our ideas about grief and to experience it as it actually is. But I find it so difficult to be with things as they are! To be with Rebecca as she actually is. Some days it's excruciating just to be inside my own skin. A lot of men have this trouble.

I continued, "Maybe this noble quest for spiritual emptiness and freedom presents a new opportunity for the practice of men's frontier spirit and courage. Perhaps we have a paradoxical calling, to be warriors, yes, but now warriors motivated by a great immanent and transcendent love. Do we have the courage to take on such a vow? Can we take up the weapons of virtue and fight our own demons, for love? It's time we stopped seeing the enemy as only 'out there.' We've got to stop seeing those who are different from us as the enemy."

"Exactly," shot back Eckhart. "That is why I always said we cannot find God in differences, in 'this and that.'"

"Oh," I replied with surprise. "I was never fully sure what you meant." I was learning that one could not have a conversation with someone like Eckhart without discovering something new.

I didn't know if Eckhart could swallow the notion of spiritual warriorship, so I offered, "Let me put it this way. The day after Rebecca died, I shared my thoughts with a group at the Buddhist-Christian conference: I offered, 'Today I say to God, "You gave her to me and now I give her back to You."'" Of course, I was angry at God too, but in that one moment I was a guardian Indian warrior, riding bareback through a storm of grief, meaninglessness, and self-doubt, declaring a truth to which I was willing to give my life."

"So," replied Eckhart, nodding, "God is the Warrior in you."

"Yes," I continued, sensing that we were on the same wavelength. "I so appreciate your emphasis on surrender and letting go. I even love the sound of the German term you used so often: *Gelassenheit*. In *Gelassenheit*, everything is born in us. That's what you meant when you said we are each meant to give birth to God. For postmodern men, letting go means a willingness to face our vulnerabilities and our need for intimacy with a strong spirit, from God. Rather than hiding behind our moral certainties, we need the courage simply to ask for help, and to give it freely. We need spiritual practices and communities that support these subtle, complicated virtues.

"I am circling around this issue of detachment, especially for men. If we are emotionally detached when our children come to us, hungry for recognition, they may wander into a no-man's land from which they can never escape. It is important that we take the time simply *to be* with our children and to listen to them. After all, they come to know themselves by seeing themselves reflected in our eyes. Gradually, they form the self-understanding that 'I am loved. My parents and guardians want to know what I am thinking and feeling, not in order to manipulate me, but simply because they want to know me and love me.' Gradually our children see that we love them and would give our lives for them, and that is how they come to be *persons*. They come to know themselves as precious and unique because we treat them that way. If we detach from them emotionally, they will be self-less in a pathological sense, without loving attachments to enjoy or to surrender. The resulting inner desolation is true nihilism. The false selves which abandoned children construct in order to cope with life are a poor substitute for authentic living. We must have a self in order to surrender it to God.[52] Too many of us fathers have abandoned our truly masculine responsibilities."

I was thinking about how my Buddhist and Christian teachers so often criticized the whole idea of attachment as an inferior thing, and I wanted Eckhart to agree that reality is more complicated. "Two of my favorite psychologists, John Bowlby and Daniel Stern, have written beautifully about how important our early love attachments are.[53] If parents detach from their children emotionally, the children become invisible, even to themselves. Their self-esteem is low, and they are prone to think something is fundamentally wrong with them. Bowlby describes what happens when a child, from fifteen to thirty months, is separated from the primary care-giver, from a relationship that had been secure: After a short period of his mother's absence, the child alternates crying and angrily demanding the mother return. There is hope within the child's protest. Eventually, if the mother still does not return, the child's protests fade and he becomes quieter, as though internally preoccupied. Then he becomes disconsolate and forlorn, with rare moments of hope. Finally, the child falls into emotional indifference, and even when the mother finally comes home, the child is curiously uninterested. For parents and other caretakers, physical and emotional detachment may be experienced as an abandonment and an evil.

"In fact, this clinical description sends shivers up my spine. It shows the emotional price that is paid when *good* attachments are severed or allowed to atrophy. So, I'll say it again: Loving attachment is a good thing, Eckhart, even for us! As a clinician, Bowlby agrees. He says, 'I regard the desire to be loved and cared for as being an integral part of human nature throughout adult life.'[54] Isn't a healthy person, male or female, always reaching out in love, forming bonds, and then surrendering them? Are not a desire, a pleasure, a mourning, and a groaning always going on in the heart of things, even within the heart of a spiritual master like yourself? These sufferings don't necessarily indicate an immature spirituality, do they? Isn't true spiritual detachment a willingness to go through the human condition, through attachment and loss, toward new, loving relationships? It is so difficult to form good attachments, especially if we have been abandoned in the past. We need courage and hope. I pray God will help us."

Eckhart listened patiently and carefully. I felt he was enjoying the dialogue. Then he added, "Yes, many of these questions had not yet appeared in my age. They are serious, important questions." Then he touched me and smiled. "I am sure God will help us, but I hope we do not make the mistake of using God to sanctify what we already know we want. I once found it necessary to say to my parishioners, 'You behave as if you transformed God into a candle, in order to find something; and when you have found what you looked for, you throw away the candle.'"[55]

We laughed as I nodded in agreement.

Then he added, "We should not make ideologies and dogmas out of these insights. Your love for Rebecca is bringing you into a deeper dimension of suffering in God—that is what is important. Stay in your own experience rather than seeking to make abstract principles to follow. God is free of any thought about attachment and detachment. That freedom is being born in you in an eternal *Now*."

"Right," I answered, "and Rebecca is a part of the great stream of freedom, presence, suffering, and joy running through the middle of *Now*."

He nodded. "*Now* everything is being worked out perfectly in God. *Now* is our home country, my friend."

Grief as Christian Conversion

The Eckhart Lecture

When I gave the Eckhart talk at the *Ruah* spirituality series in October, I remembered that Rebecca and the grief were nearby. I had put together the Eckhart lecture in a prayerful mood. Seeking to explain Eckhart's implicit developmental spirituality, I was over-prepared in the dimension of pure information. But Rebecca's quiet presence reminded me to stay close to Eckhart as a friend. Moments before the lecture, I sat alone in a dark chapel where two white candles burned atop an empty altar. I saw Rebecca on the table, naked under the bright light, trying to get her breath. I saw her on the cross, and I saw her next to me as I spoke. Staying close to her was simultaneously staying close to Jesus and to Eckhart. With her at my side I could not help but tell the truth. I never knew Rebecca, Jesus, or Eckhart as embodied, conversing persons. Now, they were all *physically* absent. But in knowing, touching, and loving Rebecca, I simultaneously met others in history who lived in God's love. From God's point of view, all lived. A clarity descended upon me as I walked out to greet the audience. I felt supported by compassionate, invisible presences.

As I sat in the front pew, waiting to be introduced, a continuous flow of self-conscious and fearful thoughts parted before my whispered prayer, "Thank you for this good man Eckhart. Help us to have fun talking about him. Thank you, Rebecca." When I arrived at the lectern to deliver my prepared lecture, I turned the pages of the text face down and simply spoke spontaneously about Eckhart as if he were a spiritual friend I wanted everyone to know. Emphasizing his notion that we are each called to "give birth to Christ," I was amazed to find myself utter the words "love" and "being in love" many times. I usually avoided such vulnerable words in public. But the room seemed bathed in a safe, clarifying light. Time itself surrendered its usually insistent, forward motion. I and my listeners had come upon a field of grace, into a place of Dwelling with Eckhart. As I looked at the people and they looked at me, I sensed waves of pure, safe, loving Presence breaking over us in the rhythms of our breathing. All of us would die, but in this one moment a clear, eternal, healing, loving-kindness carried our mutual presence to one another and beyond.

At first, I didn't know what to make of this extraordinary sense of Presence. Was I was being sentimental and naïve or, alternatively, really seeing things as God sees them? Was this experience wishful thinking—an example of Freud's regressive "oceanic oneness"—or a genuine mystical vision? Was I experiencing an altered state of consciousness, a liminal awareness of sacred realities, or merely a very focused state motivated by fear and anxiety? Which of these stories was most true?

The theological anthropologist in me whispered, "The key indicator of psychological distortion is that reality, with its multiplicity and its mix of the known and unknown, the controlled and the uncontrollable, violence and grace, is *suppressed*." Here was an operating standard of judgment for mystical experience. True spiritual oneness transcends distinctions, but it does not obliterate them. I could see clearly that each person in the audience was different from me, each one having an experience particular to his or her personal history. And yet, when the talk was over, several people said that they too experienced a unity of Presence. Self and other continued to exist, but a great power or energy had enveloped many of us. It seemed as if we all stood in the light of a graced timelessness, together.

Such moments happen every day when we are awake to God. In God, opposites such as self and other, past and future, light and dark, sorrow and joy, are bathed in another, subtler light which makes no distinctions. I remembered again Jesus' words in the Gospel of John, "I am in my Father and you in me and I in you" (John 14:20). For a Christian, this intersubjective experience defines reality. We see what is apparently different from us more clearly when we love with unselfish love. Then we find we are not so different from one another after all. Perhaps, by necessity, a direct perception of this Reality behind reality is a kind of altered state, altered from our everyday consciousness of habitual fear, judgment and self-concern.

Perhaps our ability to see things compassionately as they are, no matter how ugly, is what forms the essence of a restored human condition, the essence of Eckhart's and Jesus' teachings. In the back of my mind resounded the words of James Agee in his *Let Us Now Praise Famous Men*. We are gifted to see that

> a street in sunlight can roar in the heart of itself as a symphony, perhaps as no symphony can: and all of consciousness is shifted from the imagined . . . to the effort to perceive simply the cruel radiance of what is.[56]

I loved his phrase "the cruel radiance of what is." I had been tempted to give an upbeat, academic lecture, setting myself apart from the audience, being an expert who possessed knowledge that others didn't have. But Rebecca kept inviting me into the truth of the moment with others. Deep sorrow and the infinite joy of God's Love were the touchstone of my relationship to Eckhart, and to the audience in that moment. The "cruel radiance" of the cross within me sought to commune with the cross in others, and in that meeting, joy arose. In the lecture, I could have merely mined this curious, medieval friar for some of his poetic gems. But in the contemplative communion of the moment, I sensed that Eckhart *cared* about how I presented him. His desire was that people let go of self-consciousness and walk into the playful field of grace with him. His desire was mine, and Rebecca's, and Jesus'. Following the Eckhart lecture, I was surprised to realize that my public life was being transformed. Even in my professional life I was being asked to be more open and vulnerable than ever before. It was scary, but I suddenly saw that living into the radiance of each moment with others tapped a tremendous, joyful, and healing presence within me and within others. I had never felt so alive!

A New Understanding of "I" and "Thou"

Rebecca's death had thrown open a doorway in my soul. It was like stepping up to the edge of the Grand Canyon for the first time. I had never imagined there could be so much space, so much otherness, and so much mystery. My little ego had thought that its self-centered view of things was the way things really are. But suddenly I was standing in the midst of a great unknown Source from which proceeded all meaning, life and death. I couldn't see that Source directly—my senses were mediating Something to me. But I trusted Jesus' and Eckhart's vision that this benevolent Something was really there, within me and among us in creation.

How to characterize this immanent Source? Was it what countless generations of Christians had called the Son, or the Holy Spirit, or was it the ultimate Mystery, the Father? Was it the Emptiness of the Buddhists, the Tao of the Taoists, or the Empty Godhead of Eckhart? Or was it the passionately loving Thou of St. Bernard, Julian of Norwich, and St. Teresa of Avila? Perhaps it was all of them, as my spiritual friend St. John of the Cross intimated. In his fifteenth-century work "The Living Flame of Love," he saw no contradiction between God as a fathomless "abyss" and God as a very personal, passionate lover.[57] For John, our souls too, being made in God's image, are both lovers and chasms of mystery.

Rebecca's death shattered any calm expectation of life's ultimate predictability and justice. Yes, I could trust that, for me, Jesus was the Way, but now I perceived our relationship as a Wayless Way. In a sense, I had been blinded. Now I would have to extend my hands into the darkness in each moment, trusting that Christ would lead me through the gathering darkness. If I gave my eyes to Christ, would Christ do the seeing in me? This realization brought both fear and joy. Fear, because I was so used to taking control of events without God, and I didn't know if I could really allow myself to be emptied and guided by God. And joy, because I sensed a new clarity and power of seeing and listening arising within me. In the very shadow of meaninglessness, ugliness, and tragedy, an Unmoving gentle light shone on the moving way ahead. I reread the prologue of the Gospel of John:

> In the beginning was the Word, and the Word was with God, and the Word was God. He was in the beginning with God. All things came into being through him, and without him not one thing came into being. What has come into being in him was life, and the life was the light of all people. The light shines in the darkness, and the darkness did not overcome it. (John 1:1–5)

This Light did not reveal itself to me in a permanent way after Rebecca's death. I had little control over when or where grace would come. St. John of the Cross had taught me that grace was a matter of glimpses, morsels, and touches in the dark. In those graced moments I saw, heard, and touched everything—fellow adults, children, cats, trees, rocks, rivers, pews, and pencils as extraordinary manifestations of God's presence. Images of light and dark abounded in my mind's eye. I no longer had a clear sense of who I was. Who in me was doing the seeing, listening, feeling, and touching? Groping forward in complete darkness, I nevertheless sensed where I had come from, where I was, and where I was going. Grief hauled me down out of the clouds of hopeful fantasies and delusions I had concocted to cope with life. Coping was no longer an option. And yet, though Rebecca's death sometimes painted my life as ugly, transient, and hopeless, I felt simultaneously free, clear, and peaceful. While the night and the pain remained, infinite Light and consolation poured into me and into everything and everyone around me. Just as Jesus' death on a cross had released the Holy Spirit into all things, earth's winds had distributed Rebecca's ashes and beautiful presence everywhere.

Sometimes, it seemed that a personal, luminescent Thou shone out of each individual person and thing, revealing it as it really was. I was astounded to see that Light in people whom I might have heretofore considered repulsive, hopeless, sick, dangerous, or merely unremarkable. Each morning I recited in thankful whispers a version of Psalm 139:

> Darkness is not dark to you,
> The night is bright as the day.
> Darkness and light, to you,
> are both alike.

I had entered the year as a neophyte Christian burdened with a premonition of death. Fear seemed to motivate my every act. Self-reflection, prayer, and meditation alone seemed powerless when the fear of death came upon me. I thought God himself was helpless in relation to the fear. Even though I hated to admit it, in retrospect, the canyon trip was a flight *from* that fear.

But the canyon trip was also more than that: I had embarked on a pilgrimage rooted in ancient Christian spirituality. In the mystical tradition of the Song of Songs, I went out looking for a God who calls but cannot be found. Then, without knowing it, a strength had come into me, helping me to face what was ahead. Now, three months after Rebecca's death, I was more convinced of my Christian identity and had resumed daily morning prayers. Perhaps I was beginning to see the world through prayer as much as through my mortal eyes, through the archetypal soul-doorway of the Self as much as through the bodily senses.

When the inward place of decision making shifted out of my fearful ego toward the Light of Christ, I approached personal problems in new ways. For example, in the year before Rebecca arrived and in the first two months after she died, I was obsessed about my career. But by November, I noticed a relaxation in my psyche and soul. I thought less about *what to do* and more about *what I was*, and about where I felt *drawn*. What did others want from me? What gifts were being called out of me?[58] In the past, I had not been a great letter writer. But often now, something in me called me to write a letter to a particular person. The small, *doing* mind would often rebel: "You don't have time for that. Look at the things on your desk that need action. You don't know him well enough. He won't understand your motives." And so on. But apparently my soul knew! And the letter went out. Some deep part of me was responding on a level that bypassed the critical, workaholic, sometimes cynical intellect.

My mind couldn't grasp the paradox that while I was happy to be increasingly dependent on the God of Jesus Christ, I also feared bringing the Jesus story too explicitly into my story. I didn't want to talk with religious types who looked for the right buzzwords. I knew my fundamentalist friends wouldn't understand that sometimes Jesus Christ need not be named, because he is thoroughly infused in all things. They often looked only to the naming, as if that accomplished everything. If you could say yes to the question, Have you accepted Jesus as your personal Savior? then you had all your bases covered. But I felt there is a Jesus Christ who surpasses our powers of comprehension, one who is *implicitly* present in everything, because, as St. John had said, all things are being created through him. In this Jesus' Presence, all religious categories and self-conscious naming fall away into a graced Light of being. Religious beliefs and dogmas seem like small boats up there, splashing about on the surface of the soul.

The grieving process helped me to recognize the contrast between the voice of my ego and God's calling. Day by day, the distinctive qualities of the ego were revealed: Ego liked to be right. *It* liked to appear perfect. *It* liked to win. *It* wanted everyone to praise it. *It* did not like being vulnerable or dependent. *It* preferred to treat nature and others as objects rather than subjects. *It* preferred the impersonal, surface presentation of all things and beings, treating everything according to its use-value rather than its being-value. *It* liked theological thinking better than actual prayer. *It* used phrases like "Are you detached?" and "Are you Saved?" as judgments and even bludgeons. *It* liked thinking *about* and talking *about* Jesus, God, or Buddha, rather than meeting them face to face. *It* liked talking *about* love rather than actually loving or receiving love. Eckhart, Henri, Jesus, and Rebecca understood the difference between the ego and the larger Self, rooted in God's own Subjectivity. I leaned on them for support.

Gradually, I realized that the ego is not an enemy to be conquered, controlled, or suppressed. One must simply be wise to the fact that spiritually, the ego cannot be trusted to guide itself in Godward ways. It cannot circumvent its own principles of self-interest. Spiritual progress is not about suppressing this self-interest, but rather about allowing the ego's natural interests to become transparent to God's Presence. Surrounding and within the ego-*It* is a transcendent Presence which has deeper, wider and more transpersonal interests. This Presence is entirely within us, but not ours. He/She is intimately connected to the soul-doorways and presences of other persons and of nature. He/She is a Thou who loves us so intimately that we cannot step back and see Him or Her objectively. There is no other place to step *to*. This particular Thou knows us better than we know ourselves and loves us more than we can love ourselves.

This inward, transcendent Source of life and ultimate intent cannot be an object of our awareness. It is rather a powerful and elusive Subjectivity *within* our subjectivities. When we surrender ourselves and become detached in the proper way, our senses become God's, because we have turned them over. Then it is not *us* seeing, hearing, and touching someone, but God-in-us seeing, hearing, and touching someone *through* us. Even as this Thou is grounded in our souls, He or She sees the whole of things, from everyone's point of view at once. Within this Holy Subjectivity, all things are connected through Love, and when we see with the eyes of this Love, it is Love itself seeing things through our eyes.[59]

One day, a Buddhist friend asked politely if I had direct experience of this Thou as something separate from me, or whether it might be an imaginative image that I employed. He himself could find nothing like it in his experience. I said that Thou was an experience, but not of the objective sort. Reaching down beside my meditation cushion, I picked up a wooden striker and hit a large brass bell. Its deep rich tone hummed for about a minute. Then I said, "If I sit here and merely look at the bell, I might perceive many beautiful things about it. But I never hear a sound. In like manner, if I sit in silence and never speak to Thou, I will never hear a response. This I–Thou relationship is direct experience, but it is experience that arises out of faith. If one doesn't act in faith, one doesn't have the experience."

My friends, Henri, Marg, Rebecca, and Eckhart picked up the striker of faith too. Our love-network crossed the line of living and dead, revolving around an invisible, interdependent light of Presence. While our egos stood at a defensive distance from others and nature, this Presence conveyed a participation in a deep, interconnected web of being. When we brought our personal experience into the light of this Presence, all things passed through.

I was becoming more confident in the view that from within this Presence within us, seeing and being seen are simultaneous events. Eckhart once wrote that

> The eye in which I see God is the same eye in which God sees me. My eye and God's eye are one eye and one seeing, one knowing and one loving.[60]

The ego wants to see things only from its small point of view. *It* wants to control everything from its own perspective, excluding others' participation and freedom. The Holy Thou's interests, by contrast, both include and transcend our own. From Thou's point of view, my liberation and the liberation of others and of nature are simultaneous events. My loss is everyone's, and theirs mine. I can only become free as others become free, and vice versa. This Thou cannot be a lonely, Mount Olympus God. God is loving God in us and through our relationships. Our role is to surrender into that loving dance and to express it.

I heard Eckhart's words of God's free mutuality as a rough equivalent to the pivotal motto of the modern 12-Step movement: "Let go and let God." But it was clear I needed God's help to know the appropriate moments for letting go versus moments for holding, protesting, creating, or declaring. I could ask God to help me. The Light would shine in the darkness whether I was thinking about Rebecca or not. Could I let that confidence pervade my inner life?

East Meets West, in Jesus, in Me

The psychic struggle between taking hold or letting go appeared consciously for me when I first encountered Eastern spirituality. In the fall after Rebecca's death, a dream reminded me of the East-West culture shock I had experienced as a young man. One October night I dreamed I was teaching Sam karate. We sparred, making aggressive moves against each other, but our sudden extensions and swings of hand, foot, and body were accompanied by laughter. Occasionally we broke into playful wrestling.

When I awoke, I remembered how, in 1967 as a Dartmouth undergraduate, I was introduced to Taoist meditation and Korean *Tai-Kwan Do* karate. In the winter our teacher took us outside to walk barefoot in the New Hampshire snow. This practice was meant to break our habitual aversion to cold. We were to "become one" with the snow, warming our feet with *chi,* the bio-spiritual energy of the Tao within us. I was astounded to discover that it worked, not by an assertion of will as much as by a surrender of will to a power that was both within me and transcending me.

The Tao was in me and I was in the Tao. Prior to these experiences, I didn't realize "I" could contain energies and wisdom of which I was not conscious. An intellectual conflict arose: On the one hand it seemed I was "taking hold" of my life, making something of myself. I had envisioned an Ivy League education, had made it happen with the help of scholarships, and had then completed it without my parents' support. I was proud of the personal effort and the results. But when I stopped to look closely at this taken-for-granted "I," as suggested in Eastern meditation techniques, it seemed to be a storehouse of ancient and new mysteries over which I had no control. Which self-perception, which worldview, was more true? Was the "I" of the up-and-coming Dartmouth government student something substantial and trustworthy, or not? It seemed to require an either-or choice.

In the Lutheran environment of my Wisconsin childhood, ego-surrender was not popular. Yes, one must be a follower of Jesus, but in one's work life and relationships, in all the practical matters of everyday life, the conscious ego and its willful strategies went unquestioned. Luther's famous cry, "Here I Stand," reinforced fierce individualism among churchgoers, in relation to others and, sometimes, to God. Lutherans in mid-Wisconsin, circa 1950s, presented an outwardly friendly, but privately guarded, suspicious, and sometimes hostile attitude toward Roman Catholics. The pope appeared to be demanding depths of spiritual surrender that violated personal conscience. We Lutherans carried the implicit, stereotypical belief that Catholic parishioners had allowed themselves to be neutered and hypnotized. They had become spiritual sheep! Once, in high school, I had walked into the back of a Roman Catholic church while a High Mass was in progress. I saw the thick, blue-and-white clouds of incense ascending above the gold and red altar cloth. Two unsettling inner voices vied for my allegiance. One voice said, "Look at this Mystery! There is a wonderful depth here." And the other replied, "Oh nonsense! The priest is a huckster, a Wizard of Oz pulling the levers of hypnotic mass control. These people are zombies, merely doing what they are told. Don't fall for it." The latter voice seemed more familiar and won the day. I wasn't going to get lost in any mysteries. I knew exactly who "I" was. I was a sinner in God's eyes, but he loved me still and was proud of my efforts.

Dartmouth was steeped in the humanist tradition of the Enlightenment. Neither Catholic mystery, Lutheran piety, nor Taoist "flow" was welcome in the classroom. To surrender my taken-for-granted "I" or ego would have to be a private undertaking. I was attracted to the idea that "I" was more than I knew. But believing that some unseen power in me could warm my bare feet on the snow was like taking a place at the smoky Roman altar. Still, I did it. Taoism and Zen were exotic, refreshing alternatives to Christian religion. In the 1960s, the works of Alan Watts, D. T. Suzuki, Herman Hesse, and Lao-tzu were popular on college campuses. My own Christian religion seemed hopelessly anachronistic, its ideas and practices unable to bear the exciting promises of modernity, the depths of psychic and psychedelic experiences being uncovered daily, and the political catastrophe of Vietnam's escalating horrors.

Both Taoism and Zen highlighted the healing and revealing powers of nature. I had never heard of such a thing in the Lutheran church. There, everything good came from Jesus and a literal reading of scripture, and everything else was irrelevant. Lutherans offered an entirely person-centered, Jesus-centered spirituality. But I knew intuitively this wasn't the whole story. As my parents' relationship descended into alcoholic chaos, I often went into nature to wander among the trees, looking for birds, partridges, deer, wood ducks, and an occasional black bear. Sometimes, in my loneliness and rage, I killed whatever I found. But usually I moved in the forest's shadows, listening for invisible presences, like a monk listening for the still, small voice of God. I could believe the Taoist notion that there was an intelligence in nature and that our task was to live in conformity with that intelligence. Having grown up in the snowdrifts of northern Wisconsin, I knew snow in my bones, even before the Taoist teacher directed my bare feet there. When I walked on snow I walked on the floor of my real home. True spirituality included and transcended both nature and persons.

Believing that the older generation and the received dogmas of traditional religion were hopelessly corrupt, manipulative, and judgmental, I drank in the refreshing Eastern message that Nature was inherently nurturing and welcoming. I read:

> The Tao gives birth to all beings,
> nourishes them, maintains them,

cares for them, comforts them, protects them,
takes them back to itself,
creating without possessing,
acting without expecting,
guiding without interfering.
That is why the love of the Tao
is in the very nature of things.[61]

Each karate lesson began with silent meditation on individual cushions, "to center our energies in the belly and in the earth." We were instructed to surrender control of our breathing to the powers of Nature arising within us. Slowly I learned that our sparring and breaking of bricks expressed not a willful urge to dominate opponents or nature, but rather a concentrated, artful expression of the universal power of *chi*. I pondered this intriguing Eastern notion, that one could "win" by surrendering.

Meanwhile my studies in the Government Department at Dartmouth were based on Western principles of logic, humanism, competition, and dominance. While the coursework trained me to fragment my life into unrelated chunks of information and intellectual categories which could be used to further my career, karate taught me how to bring my body, mind, and spirit back into unity. I originally majored in government because I hoped for political resolutions to the world's suffering. If my purely cognitive studies of these political realities eventually depressed me, the Taoist meditations in the snow and the spiritual choreography of Korean karate brought hope. In those days the airwaves and newspapers overflowed with images of the Vietnam War. But each day, in going to the cushion and in bringing awareness to the flow of breath, inward and outward, my spirit was revived.

As an undergraduate, I had no inkling of unconscious motivations. I thought my consciousness defined reality. In my conscious mind, I had left Christianity behind. Now, over twenty years later, I realized that even in those college days, my understanding of Taoist and Zen teachings secretly nourished and was nourished by the life of Christ in me. I thought I had gone away from Jesus, but he was still there, walking, learning, and blessing with me, within me.

On the wall that rose up from the foot of my grandparents' basement staircase, there hung a picture of the shepherd Jesus carrying a lost lamb back to the flock. When I was a child, I always had to walk down those stairs to get to the basement bathroom. As a result, the Good Shepherd was permanently imprinted in my soul: not merely his image, but something of his being. In spite of my conscious rejection of the Christian religion as a young adult, Jesus was invisibly there within Lao-tzu's words, "comforting, protecting, and taking me back to himself, acting without possessing and guiding me without interfering." Grieving was an ever-deepening surrender to the Tao-in-Christ within me, more and more becoming my way of being with others.

After the dream about Sam and karate, I reflected on how Eastern spirituality was now woven throughout my Christian life in innumerable unseen ways. Rebecca certainly was a gift from God and the presence of Christ (Christian). But she was also an expression of the beautiful Tao, and "just this," one precious person in the cosmic web of "inter-being" (Zen). I saw that, in the words of the Buddhist teacher Thich Nhat Hanh, Rebecca, Jesus, Eckhart, and I "inter-are" forever.[62] Rebecca, like Korean Zen's *Kwan Yin* and Jesus' mother Mary, comforted, expected nothing in return, gave all life, and was now everywhere present, in the very nature of things. Kwan Yin means "The One Who contemplates the sound of the world." She hears and responds to the Suffering within our sufferings. Gradually, for me, Rebecca was joining Kwan Yin and Mary. I was becoming more comfortable with naming the All, the Tao, *my God*—the same God that Jesus Christ knew and loved. Jesus was so personally in love with this Beautiful, Loving Mystery that he preferred to use an intimate term like our "Daddy," when he prayed. Now, my experience of God came through the name "Daughter," my Rebecca. I heard the sound of the world through her.

When I said "Thank You" to God, I believed God heard me, delighted in me, and said "Thank you," in return. Likewise, when I surrendered to God, God gave me back myself. The grateful surrender and the return were one movement. I saw no contradiction with my Taoist and Buddhist experience. Didn't the Tao also hear and echo my Thank You? Weren't emptiness and compassion two faces of the same thing in Mahayana Buddhism, just as suffering and love were two faces of the same thing in Christian contemplation? All these spiritual ways had instructed me in the root discipline of surrender. In the surrender, all opposites were reconciled in the Whole, in God.

The spiritual traditions that fed me, both East and West, suggested that my true Self was hidden in a larger Presence which moved within and beyond conscious purposes, personal ego, and will. Each path, in its own way, counseled me to give up trying to achieve ultimate meaning and peace by my own efforts. Each pointed out that I was more than my thoughts. By my own thinking and will, I could not have conceived Rebecca, carried her, prevented or accepted her death. The smaller, ego self can fight with reality, trying to figure events out in the hope of mastering them. But this is the way of inevitable defeat, bitterness, and cynicism. The great spiritual traditions, East and West, counsel the wisdom of letting our intellect and desires be shaped and used in service of the Mystery who bends toward all creation in mercy and love.

Rebecca's Due Date: November 17

On November 17, Rebecca's due date, Marg and I drove to the cemetery to be with her. Along the way we stopped at a florist to get flowers for the grave. A cold, overcast sky released a light, steadily descending cloud of snow flurries. The first snow of the season. I hadn't been feeling much until I noticed the snow. Something from heaven, I mused. Then irritation and impatience bubbled to the surface. The florist, alone in her shop, took at least ten minutes to find four white roses. "What is she doing, growing them?" I asked Marg. I noticed my jaw was set tight and my lips were pursed. I wondered if I were angry, but I couldn't see what it was about.

Marg told the woman that she didn't have to wrap the flowers because we were going to use them right away. But the florist insisted that the weather outside was freezing: if the roses weren't wrapped, they would die. She wrapped them. We got back into the car. Marg was driving, silently. She seemed inside herself, unavailable. Again, the irritation worked its way into my back, fingers, and toes. Marg was taking forever to back up and turn out of the driveway! Finally I blurted out, "Can't we get moving?" And then, "I'm sorry. I'm a bundle of nerves. Reminds me of the afternoon I came to see you in the hospital. Your waters had broken and you were anxious. I have a hard time when you're anxious or preoccupied."

She replied. "Yeah. I remember that. All you could talk about was the presentation you were supposed to give at the Buddhist-Christian conference in two days. You were sitting by the window poring over your notes, trying to come up with an outline." I felt embarrassed and ashamed that she remembered my lack of sensitivity. In those very moments Rebecca had been losing her precious, protective amniotic sac.

I replied defensively, "I was just barely able to cope. I had staked a lot on doing well in my presentation. The big issue for me all year was what to do with my career. I was under a lot of pressure."

As we approached the town where Rebecca was buried, I had the eerie sense I was going to see her again, as if she were alive. Tears welled up in my eyes. Part of me watched this amazing change in my awareness, from her complete absence in the form of an abstract memory, to her imminent presence. It occurred to me that I was again on a pilgrimage. I was entering into a ritual that transcended the grasp of my intellect. I remembered some graduate work I had done on "primitive" rituals and pilgrimages. Ritual practices occasioned altered states of consciousness in which the usual structure of time and place broke open. Ritual space was "liminal," at the border between sacred and ordinary. During liminal events, eternal things seemed more real and tangible than the material things around us. Now, I was flooded with an eerie sense of being borne along by a powerful, benevolent wave of Presence. "I," in the ordinary sense of things, was no longer in control. Tears fell from my eyes as my lips formed the words, "We are coming for you." This seemed true for now and also in the sense that Margaret and I *were*, in the long run, headed for death and reunion with Rebecca.

At the graveside, snow had begun to cover the grass. I remembered how it had been raining on the day we buried her. Now, as a light snow drifted down, we placed four white roses on Rebecca's grave. Four, to symbolize the growing, nuclear family that would always include Rebecca. Marg and I stood there for five or ten minutes in silence, both of us crying. Images of the burial day floated through my mind like clouds. I remembered Rebecca's heaving chest and beautiful face. I remembered carrying her in the cotton blanket and singing to her at the funeral home. Then gradually, Marg and I began talking to each other and to Rebecca. We both said this isn't what we wanted. We told Rebecca we were sorry. "Now," I said quietly, "I understand what Jesus meant when he said to his beloved disciples, 'I must go so the Holy Spirit can come to you.' I don't know if I would be so open to the Spirit if I wasn't so terribly broken by this." I understood the resurrection in my experience now. It was not merely a sentimental idea. "Resurrection only comes when we love completely, letting it all go," I said to Marg.

As Marg and I held each other, I glimpsed a greater depth of sorrow, peace, and joy than I had ever seen in my life. Later, I reflected that I must have been in one of those liminal states. Perhaps it was being-in-love that allowed me a glimpse of the way things really are. It seemed our loving urge for reunion with Rebecca also expressed our longing for union with God, and God's for us. Through our participation in God's love, we were "really" with Rebecca, our deceased daughter. Marg and I were both on our way to our deaths and to her, and simultaneously with her already. Already and not-yet. Marg turned to me, "You know, we're with her, in a way, and yet . . . I want the real experience. I want to be with her fully, to see her again." We wanted this child so much!

We stood in the cold, in silence. I said, "She was, *is*, an outcome of our love for each other. She is the result of some whole-hearted loving, both in her conception and in her brief life inside you." Marg squeezed my hand. Just that morning Marg and I had laughed to see the new Roman Catholic catechism declare "moderate plea-sure" in sex morally acceptable for married couples. "Thanks for the permission," we had said. Now Marg replied to me, "More than moderate pleasure."

I chuckled, "Yikes, maybe that's why Rebecca died. Punishment for having too much fun!" We laughed through our tears. Seeing a crow atop the church I added, "Black Bishop, on the lookout for ecstasy!"

Another crow flew into a nearby tree. Both birds cried out inter-mittently into the silent, snow-muffled cemetery. As if suddenly thrown into a mythic, archetypal drama, I saw black ravens leaping and diving through the steady, silent white flurries.

Then, remembering that for Native Americans of British Colum-bia, ravens symbolize the Creator, I imagined that their cries were God's, and ours. From the church roof I watched myself standing by the grave of our daughter. Again and again I leaped into the sky, beating the falling snow and the thick, cold air senseless with my powerful wings. Wings of destruction, mourning, mercy, and creation.

As we looked down at our flowers lying on the cold ground, Mar-garet whispered, "White roses," and I replied "Black death." The

whole universe revolved around this cemetery, this grave, these
fresh ashes returning to the earth. I felt God's certain Presence, as
clear as black and white, each color symbolically interchangeable,
starkly different, and yet each equally transparent to a great mystery
incarnate.

Looking Into Heaven

> In the middle of Wisconsin, in the house
> that he and Grandma built after World War I,
>   the grey clouds
>   hung low. A mourning
> dove settled into the Arbor Vitae beside
>   his back porch.
>   "I took the train to New York and then
>   a troop ship
>   to the trenches,
> with a couple hundred fellas
>   from the farms around here.
>   Only twenty-six came back."
>
> On my last visit Grandpa sat motionless at
> the kitchen table, reflecting on the skin and
> bones he had become. "What can you do
> about it?" he offered. I never knew
> that he couldn't see
>   out of his right eye
> since a spark leapt into it in 1914.
>   No doctor knew
>   what to do about it.
>
> My arm around him, he tells about a time
> when I was eight years old.
>   He drove his pickup truck into the garage
>   with me riding
>   in the back,

"I'll never forget looking into
the mirror and seeing you hanging
from the clothesline," he laughs and shakes
his head slowly from side to side. "You grabbed
the line just before your head hit the top
of the garage door. There you hung,
                                        without the guts
                                              to let go."
We laugh with tears in our eyes.
Then, in silence
                        I put the side of my head
                                        to his,
as we look into the same distance,
                across the kitchen table
                        toward the door.

Conclusion: Living in Rebecca's Presence

Rebecca's simple, brief appearance has illuminated the lives of many, many people. About two months after Rebecca's death, Marg gave a beautiful, heart-awakened sermon about Rebecca at the Society of St. John the Evangelist monastery in Cambridge. Mothers who had lost children, and many who hadn't, called and wrote messages of deep gratitude to her. Marg was devastated by Rebecca's loss, and yet her ministry of love and compassion blossomed and bore fruit.

One of my writer friends, Andy, suggested that Rebecca has been to me what Beatrice was to Dante. Beatrice drew Dante through purgatory and hell, on to the beatific vision. Apparently, when Dante's editors came across the phrase "Beatrice is Christ" in his manuscripts, they changed it to "Beatrice is *like* Christ." Dante changed it back. The hairs on the back of my neck stood up when I heard that story. Dante, too, must have known the experience of glimpsing the real Christ in another. Now, when my heart opens—something that happens more often because of Rebecca—I see her in everyone. I see her innocence, vulnerability, suffering, and desire for life. Her belovedness is there, in everyone and in nature. In some way, she and others are "in Christ," a phrase St. Paul so often used. Through her I glimpse a very beautiful truth, that our being comes from and goes back to God in each moment, just as Jesus' did. We are each Light-bearers, God-bearers, becoming transparent to the qualities of God, as we approach union with God. Like Jesus, like Rebecca, each of us is destined for this epiphany and transfiguration. But, of course, participation is optional. Some of us choose to strike the bell and some don't.

Allowing myself to be broken in God's Presence has conveyed a new, deeper identity which seems unaffected by psychological and emotional ups and downs. My life must be about bowing to Rebecca and Christ in everyone, in every moment, no matter what. I frequently thank Rebecca for her gifts and wisdom, and I remember again the moment when I baptized her on the forehead with my thumb. In some way she and Christ had baptized me in that moment too: "That they may be one as we are one" (John 17:23).

My psychiatrist and clinical supervisor, Dr. Eugene Smith, was one of those who accompanied me through the grief process. He helped me discover that while I had always cared for and even loved my psychotherapy clients, a part of me had been trying too hard to *help*. Sometimes my ego had been too wrapped up in achieving results with clients. Sometimes I was not fully present with clients, but stood back emotionally, sized up their stories, and then offered them the perfect interpretation—*mine*.

Now, after Rebecca's birth and death, I am less concerned about coming up with good insights or analytical formulations for my clients. It is not a matter of turning off my clinical observations and my previous experience, but rather putting them at the service of love. More and more, I sense that the locus of personal transformation is love. If the right kind of love is there—valuing the other as a precious *other*—healing is more likely to follow. This kind of love is deeply, bodily empathic. It genuinely wants to know and to *feel*, "What is it like being you?" Certainly there are limits to what interpersonal love can do—those whom we love must be able and ready to receive it. Some of us are simply too broken to receive the love that is offered. But it is clear that healing is much more likely when we live in community with people who understand the priceless value of life and love. I realize that the mid-life crisis that had pushed me to the Grand Canyon was not about starting a new career, but rather about letting my current work and life die and be transformed. The death I had feared at the beginning of the year was not my physical death but the death of an old, familiar, smaller self.

I had struggled to understand Eckhart's phrase "suffering in God." What made this kind of suffering different from ordinary pain? Gradually, I learned that grieving in God is intrinsically relational, connecting us to something ultimate in everyone. While feeling the suffering of others more deeply is often unpleasant, it is always healing when experienced in God. This insight affected my work as a therapist. I realized I am most effective when I let-go-in-love with my clients, allowing myself to be broken with them, in God's Presence. Turning toward God inwardly, in the presence of others, allows us to see them as God sees them, setting them free. God doesn't require that we use religious language in our relationships. God wants to know if we can "walk the talk."

Making ourselves available to the suffering of others is a difficult spiritual practice. It cannot mean that we allow ourselves to be engulfed and crushed by others' actions, dilemmas, or feelings. The psychological term "codependence" describes such a person. Most psychotherapists know this joke: "What's the definition of a codependent person? A person who, when at the point of death, someone else's life flashes before his eyes." Some Christian women writers have suggested that men and women face different temptations to sin. For men, there is a prevailing inclination to isolate ourselves from intimate relationships, while for women, there is an ever-present temptation to lose themselves and their own, individual power and worth in relationships. All of us, men and women, must be deeply grounded in our personal experience as we open to the suffering of others. If we leap to the universal level of experience too soon, we obliterate the gift of our uniqueness and the special abilities, sufferings, talents, and wisdom that come with it. Boundaries are given by God and good. Each of us is given a cup to drink, the cup of our own life. And we must be awake to the possibility that the most compassionate thing to do is to let someone have his or her own suffering, just as we have ours. As the Psalmist says, "The Lord is my chosen portion and my cup; you hold my lot. The boundary lines have fallen for me in pleasant places; I have a goodly heritage" (Psalm 16:5–6). Can we accept and live our own heritage in God? In like manner, we ought not to mess with others' boundaries and the cup that they have been given. In Deuteronomy (19:14), we are admonished, "You must not move your neighbor's boundary marker, set up by former generations."

Healing love comes from God. It is not our possession. Love cannot be restrained by the leash of language. It comes from the Beyond Within, by grace. We call "it" by many names: God, Christ, the Holy Spirit, Amida Buddha, Krishna, the Presence, the One, the Beloved. Our ability to extend unconditional love requires willingness to receive it first, and then willingness to let it go out to others. It "wants" to be shared with others—that is the essential nature of the Spirit. When we do this, God in us is loving God in others. When we do this, ego conflicts, competitiveness, and self–other comparisons fall away quite naturally.

Sometimes, those of us in the helping professions need to let go of habitually *helping* others and give ourselves permission to simply *love and appreciate* them. If we can do this, gradually surrendering some distance between us and them while simultaneously staying within the boundaries of our own bodies, we will find a deeper level of healing empathy and compassion. If we are deeply rooted in unconditional love, we can let ourselves relax with others, accompanying them as if we shared their dilemmas completely—though perhaps we are a bit less afraid to be walking so close to the edge of what is known. Since Rebecca appeared, I am more confident that when we wander into the ultimate Mystery, we will find ourselves still walking, even though the ground we knew is gone. If we step off the edge, we will not plunge to the bottom of life's canyon. And, even when we suffer the ultimate threat, death, it is not the last word. There is a love that lives beyond death. This astonishing insight puts our worries about little things into perspective.

Though my work always has its painful moments, I am now more likely to look forward to meeting with clients. They remind me of who I really am—a fellow traveler with a mortal wound. I am less interested in grand theories about the relationship between our mothers, fathers, current relationships and dreams, and more interested in accompanying clients and keeping my eyes and heart open, looking for where the love is blossoming, or not. Exploring a person's history of intimate relationships is still an important part of doing psychotherapy. Making good clinical judgments about appropriate treatment is still important. But now I see more clearly that both therapists and clients can go backward or forward in time with an intention to love, or not. We can make diagnoses, treatment plans, and referrals with an intention to love, or not. We can go to a therapist or counselor intending to learn how to love, or not. Intending love, for ourselves and others, is the critical factor in emotional and psychological healing.

Gradually I have come to see how each session with a client is a poem, with a beginning, a middle, and an end. I often find myself watching each person's face tenderly, just as I watched Rebecca's. Each person is a Christ, Buddha, prophet, healer, and beloved, wanting to be born. I have become more attentive to how little births of truth, insight, and compassion enliven each session. Sometimes they come when a person focuses on the past, and sometimes when the person focuses on the present; no one can predict. No one can predict what *kind* of Buddha or Christ this person is going to be. Sometimes, as I sit with someone, I think to myself, "How are we going to get out of this difficulty? She's right—it's hopeless." I am stuck with her. But because we sit together in an invisible atmosphere of love, we often arrive at hope without going anywhere. Even when sessions end with no answers, a deeper dimension of hope cradles us. I can still find myself resisting going back to the same chair, hour after hour, day after day. But more and more I realize that if only I can get to the chair or the cushion, the field of grace might arise. Simply getting there is the key.

For much of that terrible year I had tangled with Eckhart and the Buddhists on the question of surrender. Now I look back and see some of my unconscious assumptions more clearly. I assumed letting go was a *doing*. I assumed spiritual practice was an *effort* and any good results were directly attributable to that *doing*. This is true, but only a partial truth. While authentic spiritual surrender has to be chosen and grasped, one also has to surrender the results to God. It is grace that heals, not our good intentions, insights, or advice. And grace is a free gift from the great Mystery out of which life and love arise. The practice of daily surrender to reality and to grace is a discipline based on an uninterrupted remembrance, or *taking hold*, of one's life purpose and then *allowing* it to happen. This practice requires a continual process of discernment, just as in flying an airplane over long distances, one needs to make continuous course corrections. With all our hearts, in God's company, Marg and I wanted Rebecca to live. But when that wasn't reality anymore, with all our hearts we wanted to experience her death as a source of new life and love, in God. Christian discernment becomes a dynamic process of waiting, desiring, listening, loving, taking hold and letting go, in God.

Gradually, I have become convinced that true Christian service entails a continuous act of grateful surrender. The ego often finds this commitment intolerable and will fight tooth and nail to regain control. Consequently, Christian service requires a daily discipline. The fundamental discipline is opening one's heart, even in situations where one might feel hard-hearted, contemptuous, greedy, fearful, or judgmental. Can I surrender the need to put myself or my ideas first—even if they are holy ideas—as a condition for loving another person? Can I say, or imagine saying, "I love you" to this person, without any conditions? Must I know that people are Christian before I love them completely and wholeheartedly? When the selfish ego's purposes are shed, there is only the universal movement from, and toward, liberating love. That movement is the true Christ within us. To *participate* in that movement is to be living a spiritual discipline.

Meister Eckhart taught that we must eventually let go of God for God's sake. Jesus had said, "I go so that the Spirit may come to you" (John 16:4). When someone whom we love leaves, they, paradoxically, become present everywhere. Jesus' and Eckhart's presence inspired me to let go of Rebecca for Rebecca's sake and to love others in the same way. In loving others well, we give up who we think they are and let them be who they really are, in God. In loving others well, we give ourselves to them and allow ourselves to be emotionally affected by them. And then we let them go into God, each in his or her own way.

Rebecca taught me that I am part of something larger than myself, both in this life and in eternity. She taught me to be thankful for those who have given me life. Several months after Rebecca's death, a dream confirmed this new sense of connectedness. I was driving down toward the ocean on a muddy road in the midst of a great grassy hillside. Stands of apple trees and piles of hay dotted the field. It had been raining earlier and now a fine mist fell. Suddenly a car appeared in front of me and stopped. My first reaction was anger that someone was getting in my way. Impatiently swinging open the car door, I was determined to give the guy some trouble for impeding my progress. Wearing only his underwear, he had gotten out of his car, which was now stuck in the mud. As he tried to push his car onto hard ground, others, perhaps his family, stood around, helplessly watching him. By the time I got to the man, he was up to his chin in muck. I realized he might drown if I didn't act. Planting my feet on firm ground on either side of him, I grabbed his upper body and hugged him close. Then I pulled him upward out of the mud. As he came out, I realized he was my grandfather as a younger man. Noticing his legs were bloody and broken, I cradled him in my arms, quietly explaining to others how to call the ambulance.

I awoke with tears of joy in my eyes, not knowing or caring whether I was carrying Grandpa, my daughter, my son, my wife, a client, or Christ; not knowing or caring if I was Mary, Joseph, Christ, Grandpa, or Rebecca carrying me. I was all of them. We had all disappeared into the Pietà.[63]

A deep sense of respect and love for my grandfather arose within me. He was still alive, now ninety-seven years old, living by himself in Wisconsin. Waves of sorrow, joy, and thankfulness rolled through me toward him, and toward his great granddaughter, Rebecca. Or maybe these passions were passing through them to me. I held them and they held me. When Grandpa was in his seventies he lost two of his children, my mother and my uncle. He, too, was familiar with the stark discipline of prayerful surrender. I will never forget his quiet, open-hearted, prayerful demeanor as he mourned his children's loss. It wasn't that the suffering disappeared. No. It was that his suffering had been given to Christ, and Christ, in loving him, bore his suffering in him.

When I awoke from the dream, I saw all those we love, living and dead, as kindred souls, on our way into the heart of a great, compassionate Mystery—a Mystery that bends into our lives and transforms our suffering into infinite joy.

I saw clearly, every loss is forever, but every meeting is forever too.

Notes

1. Cited by Paul Ricoeur, *Freud and Philosophy: An Essay on Interpretation,* trans. Denis Savage (New Haven: Yale University Press, 1970), 426–27.

2. Michael Diener, Franz-Karl Ehrhard, and Ingrid Fisher-Schreiber, *The Shambhala Dictionary of Buddhism and Zen,* trans. Michael H. Kohn (Boston: Shambhala, 1991), 71–72.

3. Some American teachers of Vipassana, such as Dr. Jack Kornfield, have integrated Vipassana practice with issues of interpersonal intimacy. See his *A Path With Heart: A Guide Through the Perils and Promises of Spiritual Life* (Boston: Bantam Books, 1993).

4. Thomas Aquinas, "On Daring," in *Summa Theologica* (Westminster, Md.: Christian Classics, 1948), Part. I–II, Ques. 45, Art. 4, p. 778: "Hurt does not give rise to anger unless there be some kind of hope. . . . if the danger be so great as to banish all hope of victory, anger does not ensue."

5. These verbal instructions, gleaned from my retreats with Joseph, are expanded upon in Joseph Goldstein, *Insight Meditation: The Practice of Freedom* (Boston: Shambhala, 1993); and especially in the chapter entitled "Meditation Instructions," in Joseph Goldstein and Jack Kornfield, *Seeking the Heart of Wisdom: The Path of Insight Meditation* (Boston: Shambhala, 1987), 25–30.

6. Stephen Mitchell, *The Gospel According to Jesus: A New Translation and Guide to his Essential Teachings, for Believers and Unbelievers* (New York: HarperCollins, 1991), 17.

7. *Meister Eckhart: A Modern Translation,* trans. and ed. Raymond Bernard Blakney (New York: Harper & Bros., 1941), 214.

8. The Dalai Lama, *The Meaning of Life From a Buddhist Perspective,* trans. and ed. Jeffrey Hopkins (Boston: Wisdom Publications, 1992), 49.

9. Quoted in *Zen: Tradition and Transition: A Sourcebook by Contemporary Zen Masters and Scholars,* ed. Kenneth Kraft (New York: Grove Press, 1988), 97.

10. Reported by Michael Grunwald, *Boston Globe,* 23 January 1995, pp. 1, 12.

11. *Meister Eckhart: Mystic and Philosopher,* trans. with a commentary by Reiner Schurmann (Bloomington and London: Indiana University Press, 1978), 6.

12. Romans 8:19–23: "For the creation waits with eager longing for the revealing of the children of God; for the creation was subjected to futility, not of its own will but by the will of the one who subjected it, in hope that the creation itself will be set free from its bondage to decay and will obtain the freedom of the glory of the children of God. We know that the whole creation has been groaning in labor pains until now; and not only the creation, but we ourselves, who have the first fruits of the Spirit, groan inwardly while we wait for adoption, the redemption of our bodies."

13. The phrase "refreshing tang" of otherness is adapted from C. S. Lewis, *A Grief Observed* (New York and Toronto: Bantam Books, 1961), 22.

14. Mark 10:21–22: "Jesus, looking at him, loved him and said, 'You lack one thing; go, sell what you own, and give the money to the poor, and you will have treasure in heaven; then come, follow me.' When he heard this, he was shocked and went away grieving, for he had many possessions."

15. St. Athanasius, *On the Incarnation*, in *Christology of the Later Fathers*, ed. Edward R. Hardy, Library of Christian Classics: Ichthus Edition (Philadelphia: Westminster Press, 1954), 107.

16. Matthew 27:46: "And about three o'clock Jesus cried with a loud voice, '*Eli, Eli, lema sabachthani?*' that is, 'My God, my God, why have you forsaken me?'"

17. Romans 8:35–39: "Who will separate us from the love of Christ? Will hardship, or distress, or persecution, or famine, or nakedness, or peril, or sword? . . . No, in all these things we are more than conquerors through him who loved us. For I am convinced that neither death, nor life, nor angels, nor rulers, nor things present, nor things to come, nor powers, nor height, nor depth, nor anything else in all creation, will be able to separate us from the love of God in Christ Jesus our Lord."

18. The Bull of Pope John XXII, *In Agro Dominico*, dated 27 March 1329 said that the accused "wished to know more than is necessary."

19. *Meister Eckhart*, trans. Blakney, Talk #17, p. 23.

20. *Meister Eckhart*, trans Schurmann, 5–6.

21. Eckhart, paraphrased and quoted from *Meister Eckhart: The Essential Sermons, Commentaries, Treatises, & Defense*, trans. Edmund Colledge, O.S.A., and Bernard McGinn (New York: Paulist Press, 1981), 41.

22. From Eckhart's sermon "On Detachment," in *Meister Eckhart*, trans. Colledge and McGinn, 288.

23. Quoted in *The Zen Master Hakuin: Selected Writings*, ed. Philip B. Yampolsky (New York: Columbia University Press, 1971), 50. A koan is a question that Zen students are meant to ponder until their rational mind gives up.

24. *The Study of Spirituality*, ed. Cheslyn Jones, Geoffrey Wainwright, and Edward Yarnold, S.J. (Oxford: Oxford University Press, 1986), 171. See also Evagrius Ponticus, *The Praktikos & Chapters On Prayer*, trans. John Eudes Bamberger, Cistercian Studies Series 4 (Kalamazoo, Mich.: Cistercian Publications, 1981).

25. See Akizuki Ryomin, *New Mahayana: Buddhism for a Post-Modern World*, trans. James W. Heisig and Paul L. Swanson (Berkeley: Asian Humanities Press, 1990), 105.

26. See discussion by Manjusrimitra in his *Primordial Experience: An Introduction to rDzogs-chen Meditation*, trans. Namkhai Norbu and Kennard Lipman (Boston: Shambhala, 1987).

27. Walt Whitman, "Song of Myself," in *Leaves of Grass* (Philadelphia: David McKay Publishing, 1900), 31-92; quoted lines on p. 92.

28. Pope John Paul II, *Crossing the Threshold of Hope* (New York: Alfred A. Knopf, 1994), 84–90.

29. Akizuki Ryomin, *New Mahayana,* 87.

30. Sogyal Rinpoche, *The Tibetan Book of Living and Dying* (San Francisco: HarperSanFrancisco, 1994), 204.

31. Bernard McGinn, *The Growth of Mysticism* (New York: Crossroad, 1994), 228.

32. Quoted in an article by Diego Ribadeneira and Adam Pertman, "Oklahomans Bury Victims as Toll Rises," *Boston Globe,* Tuesday, 25 April 1995, p. 8.

33. "Ae Fond Kiss," in *A Yearbook of Famous Lyrics,* ed. Frederic Lawrence Knowles (Boston: Dana Estes & Co., 1901), 106. A gorgeous musical expression of "Ae Fond Kiss is available on compact disk by Andy M. Stewart, *Songs of Robert Burns,* distributed by Green Linnet Records, Inc., 43 Beaver Brook Rd., Danbury, CT 06810 (1991).

34. Thomas Merton, *Contemplative Prayer* (Garden City, N.Y.: Doubleday, Image Books,1971), 68.

35. Meister Eckhart, "On Detachment," in *Meister Eckhart,* trans. Colledge and McGinn, 291.

36. A most beautiful description of the transtemporal presence of spiritual teachers in a particular lineage comes through Sogyal Rinpoche throughout his *Tibetan Book of Living and Dying.*

37. I later learned that Eckhart had quoted himself. See *Meister Eckhart,* trans. Blakney, 205.

38. Here Eckhart quotes himself again, from Sermon 40, in Bernard McGinn, with Frank Tobin and Elvira Borgstadt, *Meister Eckhart: Teacher and Preacher,* Classics of Western Spirituality (New York: Paulist Press, 1986), 302.

39. Ibid. Here Eckhart paraphrases himself.

40. See the whole Gospel of John, especially 5:31ff. and chapter 8.

41. Eckhart, paraphrased from *Meister Eckhart,* trans. Blakney, 204.

42. Eckhart had used the horse metaphor before. Paraphrased and quoted from *Meister Eckhart,* trans. Blakney, 205.

43. St. John of the Cross, "The Ascent of Mount Carmel," in *The Collected Works of St. John of the Cross,* trans. and ed. Kieran Kavanaugh, O.C.D., and Otilio Rodriguez, O.C.D. (Washington, D.C.: Institute of Carmelite Studies, 1979), 67.

44. T. S. Eliot, *Four Quartets* (New York: Harcourt Brace Jovanovich, 1943, 1974), 28.

45. See *Meister Eckhart,* trans. Blakney, 245.

46. Wellesley College, The Stone Center for Developmental Services and Studies, Wellesley, MA 02181-8268; (617) 283-2838. Contact them for a list of working papers and announcements of seminars.

47. See, for example, Robert Bly, *Iron John: A Book About Men* (Reading, Mass.: Addison-Wesley, 1990); Sam Keen, *Fire in the Belly: On Being a Man* (New

York: Bantam Books, 1991); and James B. Nelson, *The Intimate Connection: Male Sexuality, Masculine Spirituality* (Philadelphia: Westminster Press, 1988).

48. St. Teresa of Avila, *Interior Castle,* trans. and ed. E. Allison Peers (Garden City, N.Y.: Image Books, 1961), 166.

49. Eckhart paraphrases himself. See *Meister Eckhart,* trans. Colledge and McGinn, 60–61.

50. For example, John 8:32: "You will know the truth and the truth will make you free"; John 8:36: "If the Son of man makes you free you will be free indeed"; Galatians 5:1: "For freedom Christ has set us free. Stand firm, therefore, and do not submit again to a yoke of slavery."

51. Philippians 2:5–8:

> "Let the same mind be in you that was in Christ Jesus,
> who, though he was in the form of God,
> did not regard equality with God
> as something to be exploited,
> but *emptied* himself,
> taking the form of a slave,
> being born in human likeness.
> And being found in human form,
> he humbled himself
> and became obedient to the point of death—
> even death on a cross." (emphasis added).

52. From the standpoint of Christian spirituality, Thomas Merton once wrote something similar: "Yet before we can surrender ourselves we must become ourselves. For no one can give up what he does not possess" (*Thoughts in Solitude* [Garden City, N.Y.: Doubleday, Image Books, 1968], 31). From a Buddhist perspective, psychologists Mark Epstein and Jack Engler have written about the relationship between psychological and spiritual understandings of the self. See Epstein's "Shattering the Ridgepole," *Tricycle: The Buddhist Review* (Spring, 1995): 66–70. See also Engler's "Therapeutic Aims in Psychotherapy and Meditation," in Ken Wilber, Jack Engler, and Dan Brown, *Transformations of Consciousness* (Boston: New Science Library, 1986), 17–51. On p. 24, Engler writes, "You have to be somebody before you can be nobody."

53. John Bowlby, *The Making and Breaking of Affectional Bonds* (London: Tavistock, 1986); and Daniel N. Stern, *The Interpersonal World of the Infant: A View from Psychoanalysis and Developmental Psychology* (New York: Basic Books, 1985).

54. Bowlby, *Making and Breaking,* 157.

55. Eckhart, from sermon entitled "Every Excellent Gift," in *Meister Eckhart,* trans. Schurmann, 63.

56. James Agee, *Let Us Now Praise Famous Men* (Boston, Mass.: Houghton Mifflin, 1939, 1988), 11.

57. St. John of the Cross. See *Collected Works,* trans. Kavanaugh and Rodriguez, 569–652. I do not mean to imply that all the above terms for the Ulti-

mate Mystery are philosophically equivalent. Here I am simply speaking of an experiential integration.

58. I owe this insight to my friend Rev. Jim Lassen-Willems, who presented the idea to me in the third month of mourning.

59. Quoting St. John of the Cross in *Collected Works,* trans. Kavanaugh and Rodriguez, 638: "An abyss of light summons another abyss of light, and an abyss of darkness calls to another abyss of darkness, each like evoking its like and communicating itself to it."

60. Meister Eckhart, in *Meister Eckhart,* ed. McGinn, Tobin, and Borgstadt, Sermon #12, p. 270.

61. Stephen Mitchell, *Tao Te Ching* (New York: Harper & Row, 1988), #51.

62. For a beautiful discussion of "inter-being," see Thich Nhat Hanh, *The Heart of Understanding: Commentaries on the Prajnaparamita Heart Sutra,* ed. Peter Levitt (Berkeley: Parallax Press, 1988), 3ff.

63. *American Heritage Dictionary:* "Pietà (pyay-TAH; pee-ay-TAH) A painting, drawing, or sculpture of Mary, the mother of Jesus, holding the dead body of Jesus. The word means 'pity' in Italian. The most famous of four Pietàs by Michelangelo is a sculpture at Saint Peter's basilica in the Vatican. It is the usual referent for this term."